MUCH MORE THAN GIVING

MUCH MORE THAN GIVING

Resources for Preaching
Christian Stewardship

Roy H. Bleick

Publishing House
St. Louis

The Stewardship Bible Study, pp. 83—96, is taken from *A Life Alive unto God: A Stewardship Bible Study,* which was made available by the Department of Stewardship and Financial Support of The Lutheran Church—Missouri Synod in 1983. Used by permission.

Scripture quotations are from the Revised Standard Version of the Bible, copyrighted 1946, 1952 © 1971, 1973. Used by permission.

Copyright © 1985 by Concordia Publishing House
3558 South Jefferson Ave, St. Louis, MO 63118-3968
Manufactured in the United States of America.

Library of Congress Cataloging in Publication Data

Bleick, Roy H.
    Much more than giving.

    1. Stewardship, Christian. 2. Stewardship,
Christian—Sermons. 3. Sermons, American. I. Title.
BV772.B56 1985   248'.6   84-23867
ISBN 0-570-03951-7 (pbk.)

---

1 2 3 4 5 6 7 8 9 10 PP 94 93 92 91 90 89 88 87 86 85

CONTENTS

CONTENTS

INTRODUCTION

"Clergy burnout" is a phenomenon that has increasingly become the concern of denominational leaders. Burnout, however, is not the ultimate problem that needs to be addressed. Burnout is the result of a malaise rather than a basic illness. When one is not quite certain what the problem is, one is unable to face the problem squarely and resolve it. The frustration that results from not being able to grasp and overcome the cause of uncertainty and doubt leads to the condition that has been commonly called clergy burnout.

Symptoms

A similar uneasiness for which the root causes are not clearly defined is plaguing the church. This is revealed by such symptoms as continual loss of members by major denominations, shortage of income (causing many denominations to seek the help of professional fund raisers), the almost desperate, uncritical embracing of the "church growth" movement by denominations as well as individual parishes (to stem the tide of declining membership), the rapid rise of the modern charismatic movement (fueled by members looking for meaningful involvement), the plethora of "how to" books, etc.

On the basis of declining attendance, loss in membership, and general lack of enthusiasm for church programs, many people have concluded that the church is in trouble. Others, seeing the lack of the church's impact as a force for good on society in general, have concluded that the church is at best irrelevant and at worst useless, even detrimental. Elton Trueblood in *The Company of the Committed* approvingly quotes Karl Heim, who compares the church to a sinking ship.

The Church is like a ship on whose deck festivities are still kept up and glorious music is heard, while deep below the water line a leak has been sprung and masses of water are pouring in.

The basic illness so apparent has been on the horizon for perhaps the last 50 years.

The Problem

Sensing the problem already in 1937, famed German theologian Dietrich Bonhoeffer sought to call the church in Germany to the serious implications of being a follower of Christ. He termed the danger to the church "Cheap Grace," which he described in these words:

> Cheap Grace is the preaching of forgiveness without requiring repentance, baptism without discipline, communion without confession, absolution without personal confession. Cheap Grace is Grace without discipleship, Grace without the Cross, Grace without Christ, living and incarnate.

In a different environment, looking at results, James F. Engel and H. Wilbert Norton in 1975 asked the question, What's gone wrong with the harvest? They observed,

> Two thousand years ago Jesus faced His disciples and said, "Look at the fields—they are ripe and ready for harvest. Go, follow Me, make disciples of all nations." Now, 2,000 years later, the fields still remain ripe for harvest, but the granaries are yet to be filled. . . . there is much action but no harvest!

The real question, however, is not, Is the church being productive? but rather, Is it doing what God expects the Christian church to do? Wallace E. Fisher, author of numerous books dealing with parish life and stewardship, warns:

> The American church will either learn to address itself more responsibly to the realities of human need and the implications of Biblical stewardship or it may well become an anachronism in American society within another generation. Of course, God's work will go on through other people and other agencies in other places. Presently, the American church is under His judgment.

Thus the problem is not primarily that membership and attendance statistics are declining or that the budget is becoming increasingly difficult to raise. These are merely symptoms. Rather, the problem is that Christians do not know who they are or what they are called to be as the people of God.

The Redemptive Mission

God's great act in history was the sending of the eternal Son to earth on a redemptive mission. During the time of His incarnation on earth, Christ was engaged in the redemptive task by becoming mankind's substitute in earning righteousness and suffering punishment for sin. God is still engaged in the redemptive task. He calls together a people who are to give their lives to join with Him in this redemptive mission (1 Peter 2:9 and 2 Cor. 5:17-19). Their task is to proclaim to the whole world the Gospel. Christians need to be aware that God will not view lightly a people who respond to His call with their lips but fail to fulfill the mission He gives them. The basic problem in the church is spiritual. This must be dealt with before any significant change will take place. Merely getting more people to attend Sunday worship or to give more money will not solve the real problem. Rather we need to ask, What do those who attend on Sunday do in the world during the week?

Where is the church to discover again its mission? Since the church is formed by the Word of God, it follows that the church must learn from the Word of God what its mission is. Wallace E. Fisher writes:

> The Apostolic Witness is unanimous: every Christian, accepting the cost of discipleship, exercises Christ's ministry; the Christian community is fashioned by the Holy Spirit for the single purpose of accomplishing God's mission in the world; every person in the household of faith is set apart, and obedient to Christ, is empowered to witness, render priestly service, and share God's love.

The Role of Preaching

Through preaching God not only persuades people to repent and become disciples but also equips those disciples to be stewards who render service to Him. If the church is to regain its sense of mission and be clear about the purpose for its existence, the way must begin with preaching. Richard R. Caemmerer wrote in *Preaching for the Church,*

> If preaching speaks the Word by which God helps people, then it will always hold three things before the hearer: a plan that God has for him, God's judgment on his progress or failure in meeting the plan, and God's grace in Christ by which he is enabled to fulfill the plan.

For what purpose do those who have become God's children still continue to live on earth? How the pastor answers this question will determine the direction and content of his sermons to a Christian congregation. It is essential that every Christian, in order to be a good steward, be acutely aware of and able to answer that question correctly. The preacher especially ought not fall into the trap of thinking, as do most people who are only nominally acquainted with Christianity, that the church's duty is to make people "good." He must remember that the church has a specific mission from its Head, Jesus Christ. This mission is to announce the forgiveness of sins. We are to be His witnesses, that is, to let the world know what God is like, so that people may be led to believe and put their trust in Him and learn to love Him. This mission must be the direction and content of the preaching to a Christian congregation.

Preaching Justification

This does not deny the need to point out the way of salvation in sermons preached to a Christian congregation. After all, there may be those in the audience who have never heard of the way to be saved. It is also necessary to remind Christians that salvation is by grace through Christ. Even Christians need to be reminded that through Christ's holy life and innocent suffering and death, He has earned the right for every person to be in heaven. Because of the perverse human tendency to twist grace into works, Christians need to hear again and again that the promise of salvation is through grace and that it is grasped by faith.

In addition, such emphasis is necessary because knowing how we are made right with God also makes the life of dedication to God possible. It is an indisputable fact that sanctification flows out of justification. We are never justified in God's sight because of the "good life" we live. And the love that God has for us human beings is the only acceptable motivation for the sanctified life. If a pastor speaks to a congregation about living for Christ, he must point the members to the mercies of God, which make it possible. The model for this is the apostle Paul, who in his letters points his hearers to the things God has done for them before he speaks about what they are to do for God. (See particularly the letters to the Romans, the Galatians, and the Ephesians. In Rom. 12:1 Paul calls for a complete dedication of one's life to God. Notice how he bases his appeal on "the mercies of God.")

Preaching Comfort and Assurance

What about the need for preaching words of comfort and assurance? The contention that the content of the preaching to a Christian congregation should be directed primarily to the purpose of the Christian life on earth is not to deny the need for preaching words of comfort and assurance. Christians are not exempt from the problems of life. Because they are still in this world, though not of it, and because they are not yet perfect, they too will experience the ill effects of sin.

There is also the burden of persecution by the world that Christians experience because of their faith. Christians are not above their Lord. They will experience the same hatred and persecution that He did. Therefore they need to hear words of comfort and assurance for themselves during their earthly sojourn. They need to hear these words also so they can share such comfort with friends, relatives, neighbors, and co-workers. They need to hear and apply the comforting promises of God to their own lives so that they can share with others that our God loves, forgives, comforts, and helps His people.

The sensitive preacher, who knows his people well, is aware of the hurts and the battles they face in their daily lives. The conscientious preacher, therefore, wants to minister to the needs of his flock. However, the offer of comfort and healing from the Word of God often is more effective when applied individually than in a public sermon. Naturally, when many people in the congregation have similar needs or find themselves in similar situations, this calls for public preaching that meets such needs.

The Christian Mission as Frame of Reference

Granting that it is necessary for the accents mentioned above to be treated, it nevertheless remains true that the Christian's mission ought to be the frame of reference for public preaching to a Christian congregation. God's plan and Christ's redemptive work provide not only that we should be saved from eternal death but also that we should be saved to serve. Scripture makes this abundantly clear: "[Jesus Christ] gave Himself for us to redeem us from all iniquity and to purify for Himself a people of His own *who are zealous for good deeds*" (Titus 2:14—emphasis added). "He Himself bore our sins in His body on the tree, that we might die to sin and live to righteousness" (1 Peter 2:24; see also Heb. 9:14 and Rom. 6). God did not intend that the believer should rejoice in his own personal salvation and not live to God.

To ignore the purpose of the Christian's continued existence on earth or to preach on this subject only occasionally is to fail to minister properly to the people's need. Christians need not only to know how they have been saved or to be reminded that they have been saved but also to be enabled to serve God, and therefore God expects faithful stewardship, dedicated serving (Rom. 12:1-2; 1 Peter 4:10; John 15:1-16). "What does it profit, my brethren, if a man says he has faith but has not works? Can his faith save him? . . . So faith by itself, if it has no works, is dead" (James 2:14, 17). Recall also Jesus' warning: "Not everyone who says to Me, 'Lord, Lord,' shall enter the kingdom of heaven, but he who does the will of My Father who is in heaven" (Matt. 7:21). What a tragedy it is if the individual who has learned the way of salvation either has never grasped or else has been sidetracked from his mission of living for God.

Another reason for making Christian stewardship the subject of sermons is the expectation that pastors are "to equip the saints for the work of ministry, for building up the body of Christ, until we all attain . . . to mature manhood, to the measure of the stature of the fullness of Christ" (Eph. 4:12-13). God also tells us in Heb. 6 that it should not be necessary to lay the foundation of repentance and faith again and again or to focus attention on the simple instructions with which the Christian might be expected to be familiar by now. There comes a time when the Christian congregation should leave spiritual childhood and immaturity behind and go on to full maturity. However, if pastors continue to view Christians as babes and feed them only on "Pablum," they will not become mature Christians who diligently and faithfully carry out the mission that has been entrusted to them. Therefore, if members are continually treated as babes in the faith in public sermons, we should not be surprised that they do not become mature and productive workers in the kingdom.

This book is intended to help pastors in their public preaching on the subject of stewardship. As pastors through their sermons help members to understand the reason for their continuing existence here on earth, they will have set the stage for many of the symptoms described earlier in this chapter to disappear. Many other factors, such as history, expectations, interpersonal relationships, roles, willingness to accept change, training, etc., need to be taken into consideration before health and vigor can be restored. However, stewardship sermons can begin the process that will eventually bring into realization the priesthood of all believers. Since preachers must clearly understand the nature of stewardship if they are to help the church capture its sense of mission, in the next chapter we shall consider basic steward-ship concepts. Only as the preacher himself is fully aware that Chris-tian stewardship encompasses much more than giving will he be able to help the members of a congregation understand what they as stew-ards of God are to be doing in order to carry out their stewardship faithfully.

PART 1
CHRISTIAN STEWARDSHIP

If a stewardship sermon is only a cleverly devised means for raising money or for manipulating people against their will, then the preacher has become a fraud and a deceiver. But if in preaching stewardship he seeks to stir up faith into action that touches all areas of life, then he is on solid Scriptural ground.

What is stewardship? The Greek words *oikonomos* (house manager—translated "steward") and *oikonomia* (house management—translated "stewardship") refer to the responsibilities or actions of managing a household or business. In the primary sense, therefore, a steward is one who uses an owner's resources to manage a household or business for him. Stewardship is making decisions and doing the things necessary in order to make the business profitable.

The essence of *Christian* stewardship lies in managing resources that God has placed into our hands in the interest of a business He has entrusted to Christians to carry on for Him. Therefore, it is a mistake to conceive of Christian stewardship as a department of life or a narrowly defined sphere of specific activity, for example, pledging or giving money for church budgets.

Stewardship—Not Giving but Managing

In the New Testament, "stewardship" [*oikonomia*] is never used to designate the action of giving, much less the giving of money. *Oikonomia* relates primarily to the office of administration or management or to the implementation of a plan.

The word occurs nine times. In the parable in Luke 16:2-4, where it appears three times, most translations use the word *stewardship,* although some choose the word *job.* In 1 Cor. 9:17 the various translations use such words as *commission, task, trust,* and *dispensation.* In Eph. 1:10 *oikonomia* is translated as *a plan, God's plan,* or *dispensation.* In Eph. 3:2 the translators have chosen such words as *administration, work to do, dispensation,* and *stewardship;* in verse 9 they have chosen such words as *plan, secret plan, administration,* and *fellowship.* In Col. 1:25 *oikonomia* has been translated as *dispensation, divine office, commission,* and *task.* In 1 Tim. 1:4, because the variant reading *oikodomēn* (building up) is found in some Greek manuscripts, we find such words as *edifying* and *divine training* in addition to *God's plan* and *God's work.*

Many church members tend to define stewardship as something that refers to the giving of money to the church—pledging, budgets, etc. In the light of the New Testament usage, how could most Christians connect the word *stewardship* almost exclusively with the giving of money? In most congregations, stewardship has been "done" in the fall of the year when every-member stewardship visits, stewardship drives, stewardship campaigns, or stewardship interviews were conducted or stewardship rallies (Loyalty Sundays) were held to secure pledges for raising money to establish the budget. In many congregations that is the only time of the year when the word *stewardship* is mentioned. Oh, to be sure, the stewardship of time and talents is often made part of the presentation, but what impression remains with the people? Stewardship on the bottom line is spelled $teward$hip. Even many Sunday bulletins (worship folders) have a section called "Our Stewardship," which lists the amount received in last Sunday's offering.

Money! Money! Money!

An examination of stewardship literature produced by church bodies, as well as eavesdropping on conversations about stewardship, reveals that many church leaders equate stewardship with the giving of money.

Recent stewardship tracts issued by a major denomination include:

> Money and Me
> Money Is Beautiful
> My Money Helps
> Where Does All My Money Go?
> People Dollars

Add to this the fact that in most congregations the only time members are visited or "get called on" is during the "Stewardship Drive" or the building fund drive, when a pledge or financial commitment is sought. It is a small wonder that people complain: "All the church is interested in is money" or "The church is always asking for money."

Stewardship Definitions

Many church bodies have seen the folly of such a narrow concept of stewardship and have sought to correct it. Here are some examples of efforts to give a more Biblical definition of "stewardship" by individuals from various denominations:

There was a time when many people felt that stewardship had to do with possessions alone. Today, there is an increasing conviction that the functions of a steward reach far beyond the realm of money and actually touch all of life. Not only does stewardship have to do with possessions, but it embraces time, talents, personal and social life, and includes the very Gospel of Christ.

The basic approach to a better understanding of stewardship should show that stewardship is for *all* of life. This places emphasis on the individual's total commitment of his life to God through Christ and opens the door for response to God's calling in any area of life. The program of stewardship then consists of putting these principles into practice in our daily lives.

One of the scriptural terms which describes the divinely appointed relationship of man to God is that of stewardship. We are stewards of God. Unfortunately the term has in the usage of the church lost is broad and all-inclusive meaning and has been applied quite persistently to man's responsibility as to his temporal possessions. Most people think of Christian stewardship in terms of money rather than in terms of life. Stewardship teaching in our circles has been primarily financial. . . . true stewardship comprehends the responsibility of a Christian in all the many relationships of life. It takes into account every phase of human living. . . . all of life, and all its interests and ramifications, belongs to God and is without qualification to be placed into His service.

Stewardship isn't confined to good accounting of our money. It means serving as representatives of God, ministering as emissaries of Christ, wherever and whenever someone needs help of any kind.

What then is Christian stewardship? It is the recognition and fulfillment of personal privilege and responsibility for the administration of the whole life—personality, time, talent, influence, material substance, everything—in accordance with the spirit and ideals of Christ.

We are stewards of God's love because all we are, and have, and live has been entrusted to us by God, so that we may glorify Him. This implies that our stewardship concerns basically not only our possessions, but also our whole being and the universe we live in. But it implies that this stewardship is asked from us in the world of our daily work, our houses, and leisure time activities, as well as the corporate worship and work of the church.

This larger stewardship is not easy. It calls for the utmost of self and service. It is all-inclusive. No corner of one's life in any sphere or relationship is exempt from it. There is nothing we can be or do to which stewardship living does not apply. This is what makes it more difficult than the stewardship that is limited to a right administration of material things for Christ and His church.

Such statements well agree with the general approach and scope of the summary of stewardship in Rom. 12:1-2:

I appeal to you therefore, brethren, by the mercies of God, to present your bodies as a living sacrifice, holy and acceptable to God, which is your spiritual worship. Do not be conformed to this world but be transformed by the renewal of your mind, that you may prove what is the will of God, what is good and acceptable and perfect.

Stewardship is the responsible administration of something that has been received as a trust. As a steward the Christian is to be under no illusions about his position. He is steward and not master. He is the property manager, not the property owner. He is the one entrusted, not the one who gives the trust. Yet when the concept of stewardship is fully developed in its New Testament concept, it implies even more than trusteeship and responsibility. As T. A. Kantonen writes in *A Theology for Christian Stewardship:*

It contains the idea of partnership. The relation between master and servant gives way to the relation between friends working together for the realization of a common purpose. Thus in speaking to His disciples about their stewardship responsibility of fruitful service, our Lord says, "No longer do I call you servants, for the servant does not know what his master is doing; but I have called you friends, for all that I have heard from my Father I have made known unto you." And Paul ascribes to Christian stewards the dignity of being God's fellow workers. This partnership is furthermore the partnership of

Father and Son: "You are no longer a slave but a son, and if a son, then an heir."

Christian stewardship is a partnership with God in the business of salvation. Both the partnership and the nature of the business are beautifully described in 2 Cor. 5:18-20:

> All this is from God, who through Christ reconciled us to Himself and gave us the ministry of reconciliation; that is, in Christ God was reconciling the world to Himself, not counting their trespasses against them, and entrusting to us the message of reconciliation. So we are ambassadors of Christ, God making His appeal through us.

It is to be noted that this is not an equal partnership, since the business and all of the resources belong to God. It is also a partnership that God, not we, established. Jesus says, "You did not choose me, but I chose you and appointed you that you should go and bear fruit and that your fruit should abide" (John 15:16). The object of all stewardship activity is to use the resources placed in our hands in such a way that people come to know and trust in the only true God. God has placed in the hands of His followers the ministry of reconciliation. The following diagram may help us to visualize this definition of stewardship:

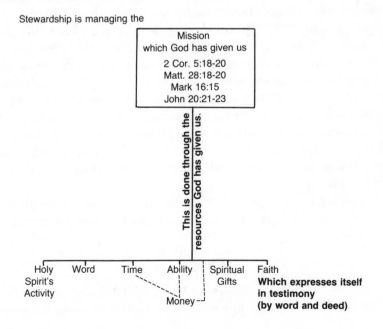

The chief object of stewardship sermons should be to give the hearers a sense of mission. Therefore, we ought to avoid speaking of stewardship in the hackneyed terms of time, talent, and treasure. The slogan about giving of our time, talents, and treasure ought to disappear from our vocabulary. To speak only of *giving* our time, talents, and treasure ignores the far greater concept of *managing*. Management covers not just a portion of the resources but *all* of them. We are to manage everything in the way God intends, even what we use for ourselves. Using the common, alliterative phrase makes it too easy for people to fall into the trap of thinking of these things as ends in themselves. It is not the money or the time in itself that is the object of the mission that Christians have been given. Money, time, and talents are merely resources to be used to accomplish the mission. They are means to an end. The mission is the ministry of reconciliation that God has committed into the hands of His believers. We would be misleading people if we taught them that the time and talents they offer in activities centered in their church building are all that is involved in their stewardship responsibility.

God has given us not only the honor of managing this important task but also all of the resources necessary to accomplish it. First and foremost is Christ's own presence among us. When He gave the commission (stewardship), He promised, "Lo, I am with you always, to the close of the age" (Matt. 28:20). And He also promised the Holy Spirit to assist us: "You shall receive power when the Holy Spirit has come upon you; and you shall be my witnesses in Jerusalem and in all Judea and Samaria and to the end of the earth" (Acts 1:8). In addition to Christ's presence and the work of the Holy Spirit, we have time, natural abilities, spiritual gifts, money, personality, contacts with other people, and things too numerous to mention. All these resources and anything else that touches our lives are to be used in such a way that God can work through us to further His mission of revealing Himself to the world as Savior.

In order to explore more fully the meaning of stewardship, we examine it in the light of God's activity as Creator, Redeemer, and Sanctifier.

Creation

One of the fundamental aspects of Christian stewardship is the realization that everything that exists belongs to God. The general

Biblical statement that covers all of this is found in Ps. 24:1: "The earth is the Lord's and the fullness thereof, the world and those who dwell therein." God lays claim to all inanimate objects: "The silver is Mine, and the gold is Mine, says the Lord of hosts" (Hag. 2:8). God also claims as His own all of the wild and domesticated animals, fowl, and every living creature: "Every beast of the forest is Mine, the cattle on a thousand hills. I know all the birds of the air, and all that moves in the field is Mine" (Ps. 50:10-11). This ownership even extends to human beings: "We are His people, and the sheep of His pasture" (Ps. 100:3). In the New Testament we are quite forcefully reminded that we do not even belong to ourselves but that in body, soul, and spirit we belong to God (1 Cor. 6:19-20). Even though we may possess many things, in reality they are all God's. He has not relinquished ownership of anything.

From Martin Luther's explanation of the First Article of the Apostles' Creed, Lutherans have learned to believe that God is gracious and allows people to use His possessions for their own needs as well as for the advancing of His kingdom. Because God is so kind and generous, the corrupted human nature, which is afflicted with inherent selfishness, tends to forget that God is the ultimate owner of all things.

As we stand in relationship to God as our Creator, we must never forget that human beings are in a position of responsible trusteeship. Anyone who has been entrusted with the property of another is accountable to the owner. Therefore, Christians must constantly be on guard and hold before their eyes the fact that misuse of God's resources or refusal to use them in His service amounts to embezzlement. Jesus once said the kingdom of God is like "a man going on a journey [who] called his servants and entrusted to them his property. . . . After a long time the master of those servants came and settled accounts with them" (Matt. 25:14, 19). As Christian stewards, we need to consider whether, when an accounting is required of our life, He will say to us, "Well done, good and faithful servant!"

In addition to being accountable for the proper use of the resources God has placed in our hands, Jesus stressed the importance of the productive and accountable life:

> I am the true Vine, and My Father is the Vinedresser. Every branch of Mine that bears no fruit, He takes away, and every branch that does bear fruit He prunes, that it may bear more fruit. (John 15:1-2)

The Christian steward constantly needs to ask himself, What is the objective of my life? What is my main concern in life? According to Jesus, the main concern should be seeking the kingdom of God—even before the necessities of life:

> Therefore I tell you, do not be anxious about your life, what you shall eat or what you shall drink, nor about your body, what you shall put on. Is not life more than food, and the body more than clothing? . . . Your heavenly Father knows that you need them all. But seek first His kingdom and His righteousness. (Matt. 6:25, 32-33)

To a large degree, Christian stewardship is a matter of priorities. It is not only a matter of how I use God's possessions, but it means putting God first in all areas of life.

Redemption

God is more than Creator and owner. He is also Redeemer. Christ has redeemed all people from their sins. However, He has not merely redeemed us *from* something; He has also redeemed us *for* something. Again, Martin Luther has captured this so beautifully in his explanation to the Second Article of the Apostles' Creed. First he describes who Jesus Christ is: "I believe that Jesus Christ, true God, begotten of the Father from eternity, and also true man, born of the Virgin Mary, is my Lord." Then he explains what He has done: "Who has redeemed me, a lost and condemned creature, purchased and won me from all sins, from death, and from the power of the devil; not with gold or silver, but with His holy, precious blood and with His innocent suffering and death." Then he gives the reason the Son of God took on human form: "That I may be His own, and live under Him in His kingdom, and serve Him in everlasting righteousness, innocence, and blessedness, even as He is risen from the dead, lives and reigns to all eternity."

The deepest foundation of stewardship is the believer's awareness that God is active in Christ Jesus to redeem and reclaim him. The Christian believes that he belongs to God above all because in forgiving mercy God has acted to reconcile him. The proper response of the believer to the love manifested on Calvary is expressed by the hymn writer Isaac Watts:

> Love so amazing, so divine,
> Demands my soul, my life, my all!

As we contemplate the costliness of the love that sought us out in spite of our sinfulness, we are moved by gratitude, repentance, and dedication to place our lives completely at God's disposal. The blood of Jesus Christ not only cleanses us from sin but works a change in us that enables the believer to serve God.

> How much more, then, will the blood of Christ, who through the eternal Spirit offered Himself unblemished to God, cleanse our consciences from acts that lead to death, so that we may serve the living God! (Heb. 9:14)

Thus the Christian sees his life not only as a creation of God but also as a new creation. The Christian is a new creation for a specific purpose. St. Paul expresses it clearly: "Therefore, if anyone is in Christ, he is a new creation; the old has passed away, behold, the new has come. All this is from God, who through Christ reconciled us to Himself and gave us the ministry of reconciliation" (2 Cor. 5:17-18).

Through God's action the believer has become a member of God's family. God is our Father; Jesus is our brother. As members of the family we are involved in the family's business—the business of bringing salvation to human beings. At a specific point in time, God sacrificed His only begotten Son in order to save mankind. He continues the business of salvation through His adopted sons and daughters now living in the world. Jesus died to reconcile people to God, and now He gives us—the believers, those who have been reconciled—the ministry of reconciliation.

Jesus has given the commission (the stewardship) to His followers in these words: "All authority in heaven and on earth has been given to me. Go therefore and make disciples of all nations" (Matt. 28:18-19). In light of this, how can anyone conceive of stewardship as merely consisting of giving dollars to the budget or even as merely doing "church work," that is, activities performed within the walls of a church building? Stewardship involves the use of all of life and the use of all our resources in such a way as to make disciples of all nations.

Sanctification

The God who creates and redeems man is also the indwelling Spirit who acts continually to empower us for Christ-like living. The church calls this Christ-like living *sanctification*. The sanctified life might well be another definition for stewardship activity.

The Holy Spirit continues to point people to the truth of Christ, to awaken them to a repentance in faith, to unite them into a redemptive community called the church, to strengthen them for life as His stewards, and to guide them in His way.

From Martin Luther's explanation of the Third Article of the Apostles' Creed, Lutherans have been taught that coming to faith and living the sanctified life depends on the work of the Holy Spirit.

When we as Christians know ourselves to be sustained by the Holy Spirit, we must declare with St. Paul: "Whether we live or whether we die, we are the Lord's" (Rom. 14:8). The desire to please Him becomes the driving force that transforms our lives. For it is the Holy Spirit who brings us today to the same conviction that the apostle expressed:

> I have been crucified with Christ; it is no longer I who live, but Christ who lives in me; and the life I now live in the flesh I live by faith in the Son of God, who loved me and gave Himself for me. (Gal. 2:20)

The Holy Spirit, using the means of grace, is the divine energizer. Through His work of conversion He not only changes people's attitudes toward God, but He also gives them the ability to carry on God's business. Holy Scripture declares: "God is at work in you, both to will and to work for His good pleasure" (Phil. 2:13). The gifts that the Holy Spirit so freely gives to believers through the means of grace make possible all the activities that make Christians good managers of God's business.

Stewardship—a Way of Life

Through His work the Holy Spirit changes a person's philosophy of life. It is this philosophy that determines our perspective. Therefore it is the Holy Spirit who helps make God's business our first concern in life.

The life of Christian stewardship is thus grounded in a dynamic relationship between God and man. A life of stewardship is the integrated response of the whole personality of man to the whole action of God. The essence of the attitude of the stewardship life is beautifully expressed in the words of the hymn:

> Take my life and let it be
> Consecrated, Lord, to Thee;
> Take my moments and my days,
> Let them flow in ceaseless praise.

Take my hands and let them move
At the impulse of Thy love;
Take my feet and let them be
Swift and beautiful for Thee.

Take my voice and let me sing
Always, only, for my King;
Take my lips and let them be
Filled with messages from Thee.

Take my silver and my gold,
Not a mite would I withhold;
Take my intellect and use
Every power as Thou shalt choose.

Take my will and make it Thine,
It shall be no longer mine;
Take my heart, it is Thine own,
It shall be Thy royal throne.

Take my love, my Lord, I pour
At Thy feet its treasure store;
Take myself, and I will be
Ever, only, all, for Thee.

(The Lutheran Hymnal 400)

The pastor will have experienced in his own life and will have seen in the lives of others that Christians do not constantly live with this high sense of dedication. The Christian is constantly at war against the sinfulness of his human nature. The child of God needs to cry out as Jesus taught: "Forgive us our trespasses."

However, Christian stewards dare not use this struggle as an excuse for lack of faithful stewardship. The punishment received by the stewards who did nothing in the "stewardship parables" teaches that so very clearly. Christian stewards need to take to heart and earnestly ponder the words of Jesus: "Not everyone who says to Me, 'Lord, Lord,' shall enter the kingdom of heaven, but he who does the will of My Father who is in heaven" (Matt. 7:21).

Evangelical Christians firmly believe that deeds do not, even to the smallest degree, play any part in justification. Works, merit, worthiness, and intention are excluded completely from this sphere. But unless faith produces works of love and obedience it is dead (James 2:14-17). Martin Luther said, "There is a beautiful agreement between faith and good works; nevertheless, it is faith alone which apprehends the blessing without works, and yet faith is at no time ever alone."

Growth in Christian Living

To help each member be a good manager of what God has entrusted to him is one of the functions of the Christian church. Pastors are God's gifts to the church to perform this service. Growth in Christian living flowing out of justification must be the main concern of the sermon a pastor preaches. Christian growth takes place through the Holy Spirit's activity in the means of grace. As the pastor seeks to help people become better stewards, he needs to remember that two things are required for growth to take place.

The first is to confront the believer with

1. God's expectation for His life;
2. the Scriptural truth that everything belongs to God;
3. the need for a personal examination
    a. of his attitude toward God's Word,
    b. of his individual stewardship performance, and
    c. of his future goals and objectives; and
4. the Gospel's strong, unequivocal promises of grace and mercy.

The second requirement for growth is a commitment to

1. living according to the will of God,
2. specific measurable objectives, and
3. a strategy for reaching those objectives.

Stewardship sermons seek to help the individual Christian consciously live every moment, speak every word, and perform every act for the purpose of glorifying God and serving to build His kingdom in the hearts and minds of people. The following chapters are intended to help busy pastors in this task.

PART 2
SERMON STUDIES WITH EXPANDED OUTLINES

The following four brief sermon studies and expanded outlines illustrate how the clergy can teach basic stewardship principles through sermons.

The first sermon presents the purpose or objective for stewardship. It reminds us that managing resources is not an end in itself. Resources are entrusted to us so that we can accomplish our task, our mission in life.

The second draws our attention to the motive for serving as good stewards: God's love for us in Jesus and the forgiveness He gives us through Christ.

The third not only reminds us that as stewards we are accountable to God but also shows us what enables us to serve and thus be ready to be held accountable.

The fourth points to the fact that God gives each Christian a gift that enables him or her to serve. Therefore, there is no excuse for just sitting on the sidelines.

The Magnificent Mission
John 20:21

Text: Jesus said to them again, "Peace be with you. As the Father has sent Me, even so I send you."

Sermon Study

Exegetical Notes

This sentence contains two different Greek verbs, both meaning "send." John's gospel uses them synonymously. Both are used to refer to the Father's sending of Christ and to the sending of the disciples. Therefore, it is wise not to stress any difference, i.e., one is a commissioning of Jesus and the other a sending of the apostles. The sending out of the church by Jesus is parallel to the sending out of Jesus by the Father. Just as Jesus was sent into the world with the authority of the Father behind His mission, so the disciples are sent to continue His work with God's authority behind their mission also.

The first verb, *apestalken* (perfect tense), emphasizes the completion of Christ's mission to earth and its continuing effects. The second, *pempō* (present tense), emphasizes that the authoritative commission is *now* being given to the disciples.

The familiar formula *kathōs . . . kagō* is also found at John 15:9 and 17:18. In the fullness of His authoritative divine power Jesus says, "And I on my part send you."

Someone has called this verse the "Charter of the Christian Church." Why does God commission the church to this mission? He so loved the world that He sent His Son to secure salvation for all. Jesus had come with a message (demonstrated in word and deed) of God's great love. Now He was going back to the Father, but that same message still needs to be taken to all people. God has chosen the followers of Christ, the church, to take it to them.

This commissioning is not limited to the apostles alone. The events in the text occurred on the first Easter evening. From Luke 24:33-35 we see that, in addition to the apostles, the Emmaus disciples were also present, as were others: "They rose that same hour and returned to Jerusalem; and they found the eleven gathered together *and those who were with them*" (Luke 24:33—emphasis added).

Stewardship Application

Particularly important for the understanding of Christian stewardship is the knowledge that every member of Christ's body, the church, shares in Christ's own mission: "As the Father has sent Me," He tells His people, "even so I send you."

It is significant that these were almost the first words Jesus spoke to the assembled followers. This is the first of three commissions given by the risen Christ; another took place in Galilee (Matt. 28:16-20; cf. also 1 Cor. 15:6?), and still another happened on the Mount of Olives (Luke 24:44-51 and Acts 1:2-11).

The Lord's apostle Peter tells us, "You are a chosen race, a royal priesthood, a holy nation, God's own people, that you may declare the wonderful deeds of Him who called you out of darkness into His marvelous light" (1 Peter 2:9). These words show us what a unique status and mission is given to all Christians (pastors and laity). The crucial question all of us must ask is, Am I carrying out this mission as a faithful steward?

How can carrying out this mission be considered stewardship? In Luke 12 Jesus had been warning His followers to be ready for the Master's return. Peter asked, "Lord, are you telling this parable for us or for all?" (v. 41). And the Lord said, "Who then is the faithful and wise steward, whom his master will set over his household, to give them their portion of food at the proper time?" (v. 42). A *steward* is one who has a *stewardship* to perform. Jesus is both the Water and the Bread of Life. As faithful stewards we are to share Him with those who need Him. This is our stewardship.

The many aspects of Christian stewardship can be explained to a person at great length so that he may understand intellectually what is involved. However, the actual yielding of his life and his resources will await the day when he is brought to recognize that he is no longer to live for himself *but for the Christ who died for him and was raised again.* This text may be just the message that the Holy Spirit will use to accomplish this in someone's life. Pray as you prepare to preach that He may use your words to this end.

Sermon Outline

Theme: The Magnificent Mission

Brief

I. It is magnificent because the one who gave the mission is magnificent.
II. It is a magnificent mission because it is God's very own mission.
III. The mission is magnificent because of those who are the object of the mission.

Detailed

Introduction

It is Easter evening. The Lord's inner circle of disciples, along with others, is fearfully yet excitedly discussing the appearance of a resurrected Jesus to some of their number. Now two more of His disciples enter and eagerly tell that they had met Jesus that afternoon on the way to Emmaus.

Suddenly Jesus Himself stands in their midst, still bearing the wounds of His crucifixion. WOW! What a shiver of terror must have shaken the disciples by so sudden and unexpected an appearance! What a thrill must have surged through their very being—fearful yet ecstatic!

Jesus eats with them (to show it was the same body they had known for years?), then He commissions them with the words, "As the Father has sent Me, even so I send you."

What does this sending by Jesus involve? When the Father sent the Son, it was to be the Lamb of God who takes away the sin of the world. That sending involved sacrifice. The sending of the Son by the Father was a giving up—a forsaking—on the cross. In contrast, the sending of men by Jesus was not a sending away but rather a calling to partnership—not a bitter cup but an enriching gift.

The Son is sent by the Father; the disciples are sent by the Son. Yet both the Son and the disciples are sent by God Himself. The Word of the risen Lord, "As my Father has sent Me, even so I send you," makes sinful men into "ambassadors for Christ" (2 Cor. 5:20).

The process, the things we do in carrying out the mission for which

God has chosen us, is stewardship. Though most people think stewardship means "giving money," in reality it is much more than that. It means managing, that is, using all the resources God has placed in our hands in such a way that the mission—that men might be saved—can be realized.

Let us consider our stewardship responsibility under the theme,

The Magnificent Mission

It will help us rightly to understand the true scope and glory of Christian stewardship.

I. It is a magnificent mission because the One who gave the mission is magnificent.

    A. He is magnificent not merely because of His miraculous appearance.

    The Lord suddenly appeared before the disciples even though the doors were locked. It was a wonderful and miraculous appearance. This ability to perform the supernatural was nothing new for Jesus. His ability to perform miracles was well known to the disciples. (You may want to cite some examples.) The miracle alone does not make the giver of the mission magnificent; others, even the apostles, performed miracles.

    B. He is magnificent not merely because of His resurrection.

    It is true, the disciples were overcome with wonder and joy at Jesus' resurrection. They never expected it. However, it is not merely His physical resurrection that makes Jesus magnificent. Others, too, had been raised from the dead: Jairus's daughter, the son of the widow at Nain, and Lazarus. Jesus Himself had raised these people from the dead. It's true that Jesus' resurrection was different; He had raised Himself from the dead. He had declared concerning Himself, "Destroy this temple, and in three days I will raise it up" (John 2:19).

    More important than the resurrection itself was the victory it demonstrated. Jesus had assumed the burden of the world's sins. He had taken the punishment for everyone's wrongdoing and was able to survive it and emerge the victor.

    C. The true greatness of Jesus—His magnificence—lies in the fact that He is the almighty God Himself. This is what makes the mission that He committed to all of His followers so magnificent.

1. Jesus is the only-begotten Son, "begotten of his Father before all worlds, God of God, Light of Light, very God of very God, begotten, not made, being of one substance with the Father, by whom all things were made." The scene in heaven shows how wonderful is the one who said, "As the Father has sent Me, even so I send you." The holy creatures around the throne do not cease to say, "Holy, holy, holy, is the Lord God Almighty, who was and is and is to come!" (Rev. 4:8). Rev. 4 goes on to say: "Whenever the living creatures give glory and honor and thanks to Him who is seated on the throne, who lives forever and ever, the twenty-four elders fall down before Him who is seated on the throne and worship Him who lives forever and ever; they cast their crowns before the throne, singing: 'Worthy art Thou, our Lord and God, to receive glory and honor and power, for Thou didst create all things, and by Thy will they existed and were created' " (vv. 9-11).

   And yet neither His might, honor, nor glory are the ultimate in Jesus' magnificence.

2. The pinnacle of Jesus' magnificence is His love and mercy. It is the love and mercy that God has shown to human beings that make Him more magnificent in our eyes than His honor and great power and glory.

   God's holiness demands that every transgression be paid for. God's grace was able to find a way to satisfy His justice and still save human beings from suffering a just recompense for their sins. Through God's mercy every sin was paid for by Jesus Christ. Your sins, my sins, the sins of every human being were atoned for by Him.

   What makes this mission magnificent is the fact that the one who gives the mission is Himself magnificent.

II. It is a magnificent mission because it is God's very own mission.

   A. Jesus was sent by the Father to be the Savior.

   1. God had promised to send someone to rescue the human race. The first such promise was made when sin and death first came into the world through the disobedience of Adam and Eve (Gen. 3:15; other repeated promises: Is. 9:1-6; 53; etc.).

2. Finally, "when the time had fully come, God sent forth His Son, born of woman, born under the Law, to redeem those who were under the Law" (Gal. 4:4-5). It was the Son, the only-begotten, who according to God's plan was chosen to be the Rescuer. And God sent Him "that whoever believes in Him should not perish but have eternal life. For God sent the Son into the world, not to condemn the world, but that the world might be saved through Him" (John 3:16-17).

3. It was Jesus' task to save the lost. He Himself stated: "For the Son of Man came to seek and to save the lost" (Luke 19:10). God was not obligated in any way to do this. Nevertheless He willingly took this search and rescue mission on Himself. In His infinite mercy He came in order to save mankind.

B. Jesus in turn sends us on the same mission.

1. Before ascending into heaven Jesus said, "As the Father has sent Me, even so I send you." Already before His crucifixion, in His prayer for the church He said, "As Thou didst send Me into the world, so I have sent them into the world" (John 17:18). There can be no doubt about it: we have the same mission. To continue the work of showing God's great love by word and deed is our mission today. In the Great Commission of Matt. 28 Jesus described the mission as making disciples of all nations. Later on, St. Paul described the mission that God handed over to us in these words: "All this is from God, who through Christ reconciled us to Himself and gave us the ministry of reconciliation" (2 Cor. 5:18).

2. Jesus went on to tell the disciples: "If you forgive the sins of any, they are forgiven; if you retain the sins of any, they are retained" (John 20:23). God has given you the power not merely to offer God's forgiveness, not merely to hold it out as a prospect, not merely to wish it for others—*you are to forgive!* When you forgive, God Himself forgives.

Is this not a most magnificent mission God has given you? The power to forgive sins is the greatest power on earth. You have been commissioned to do it. Only Christians have this awesome power.

III. This mission is magnificent because of those who are the object of
the mission.
   A. It is not because they are so worthwhile.
   We cannot truly grasp how magnificent the mission is until
   we begin to realize how revolting sinners are to the holy, sin-
   hating God. The holiness of God means His opposition to and
   abhorrence of every type of iniquity and sin. Therefore Scripture says, "Your iniquities have made a separation between
   you and your God, and your sins have hid His face from you
   so that he does not hear" (Is. 59:2). God's judgment on the
   whole human race is that "They have all gone astray, they are
   all alike corrupt; there is none that does good, no, not one" (Ps.
   14:3). How God could even want to save such filthy wretches
   who dare to defy His holiness is the greatest wonder.
   B. God did not save people who "deserved" to be saved.
   It was not that God looked over the human race, sought out
   the best He could find, and decided to save them. God is not
   trying to develop some super race or seeking the survival of
   the fittest. The words of Jesus, "Go and learn what this means,
   'I desire mercy, and not sacrifice.' For I came not to call the
   righteous, but sinners" (Matt. 9:13), teach that it is not merit
   or worthiness on the part of people that induces God to reach
   out and save. So fantastic is God's love that not even the most
   wretched sinner (an example is Hitler) is shunned by God's
   mercy.
   C. The grace of God's mercy is so magnificent because it reaches
   out even to those who hate God and don't want to be saved.
      1. Even as He was being crucified, Jesus said, "Father, for-
      give them; for they know not what they do" (Luke 23:34).
      What Jesus taught in His public ministry, "Love your ene-
      mies and pray for those who persecute you" (Matt. 5:44),
      He practiced in His own life.
      2. And then there was Saul, who "was ravaging the church,
      and entering house after house, he dragged off men and
      women and committed them to prison" (Acts 8:3). Even
      while he was "breathing threats and murder against the
      disciples of the Lord" (9:1), the Lord chose him and com-
      missioned him to build the church he had been persecut-
      ing.

What a magnificent mission! It reaches out and enfolds the most vile. No one is outside of its love, none has gone too far to be the object of its mercy.

Conclusion

The magnificent mission is ours! God has entrusted it to us.

How faithful and diligent are we in carrying out the mission? Sad to say, we Christians aren't doing a very good job. Our stewardship of the mission must be better. We need to do a better job of managing all the resources God has given us. The resurrection victory is for naught unless people believe it. Unless people hear the message they cannot believe. Unless we Christians share the message, it will not be heard.

Surely we all desire to be better stewards. We all desire to give more time and energy and resources to the magnificent mission that God has entrusted to us. How can we keep our attention and efforts focused on the mission? By remembering:

1. It is important to God and mankind.
2. God wants and expects you to carry out the mission.
3. He has given you the resources to do it.
4. You have been especially chosen by God.

Then no matter what our vocation—no matter whether it be Sunday, Wednesday, or Friday—everything we do and every hour we spend will be to the glory of God and in carrying out the magnificent mission.

Lots of Love
Luke 7:47

Text: Therefore I tell you, her sins, which are many, are forgiven, for she loved much; but he who is forgiven little, loves little.

Sermon Study

Exegetical Notes

This account is not to be regarded as a variant of the accounts in Matt. 26:7-13, Mark 14:3-9, or John 12:1-11. The features of each account are so different that they do not allow identification as one and the same incident.

Are we to understand Jesus' words to mean that the woman's love for Jesus was the cause of the forgiveness of her sins? Some people insist on this meaning, citing the natural sense of the words and the order in which they are found. Those who connect the word "therefore" with Jesus' statement that "her sins, which are many, are forgiven, for she loved much" argue that the cause of her forgiveness was her great love. When we take into consideration the complete story, verses 36-50, it is clear that the "therefore" is intended to show Simon the reason for the difference between his display of affection toward Jesus (or lack of it) and that of the woman. The last words of the verse, "but he who is forgiven little, loves little," also show the reason for this difference. Verses 40-42 have the same message. Therefore the Greek word *hoti* does not give the reason that her sins are forgiven. Her great love shows that she had many sins forgiven. In our everyday speech we often use the same mode of expression: "It is raining, for the windows are wet." It is not raining because the windows are wet, but the windows are wet because it is raining. The rain is the cause, the wetness of the windows the result of the rain.

Stewardship Application

The story of the penitent woman and of the indifferent Pharisee teaches that when the fruits of the stewardship life seem to be lacking, we must seek the cause in the lack of love. The story ought to alert all pastors to the fact that only forgiveness can produce a heart filled with love. It is this love that finds its expression in deeds done to the glory of Jesus. True, there must be knowledge of sin and a desire to be rid of that sin, for without such knowledge and desire one does not accept or receive the forgiveness. Nevertheless, it remains true that only the forgiveness produces love in the heart. The pastor who seeks the fruit of the stewardship life in the lives of his members needs to learn well the lesson of Luke 7:36-50 and to teach it clearly.

Sermon Outline

Theme: Lots of Love

Brief

I. How do we get lots of love?
II. How does lots of love express itself?

Detailed

Introduction

Are we to understand the words of Jesus, "her sins, which are many, are forgiven, for she loved much," to mean that because she loved Jesus, her sins were forgiven? (*pause*) In order to help you understand these words of Jesus correctly, let me tell you the story that surrounds the words of our text.

Jesus went from town to town preaching and healing the sick. One day he came to the town in which Simon the Pharisee and the woman lived. When Jesus came to a town, almost everyone turned out to hear him. Apparently Simon, who was one of the leading citizens of the town, was impressed and invited Jesus to his home for a meal.

While Jesus was in Simon's house eating this meal, a woman came in and stood behind Jesus. In those days when people ate a meal they didn't sit on chairs as we do, placing our feet under the table; they reclined on couches, leaning on one elbow toward the table with their feet stretched out behind them. The woman had a very bad reputation; in fact, she was a prostitute. Although it is customary in the East for people to enter the dining room uninvited and to sit around the edges and converse with those at the table, it was unheard of for such a notorious sinner, a prostitute, to enter the house of a Pharisee.

As she stood behind Jesus, she began to cry. Her tears ran down her cheeks and fell on Jesus' feet. When she noticed that her tears were making his feet muddy, she unloosed her hair and wiped the mud from Jesus' feet. People in Jesus' day wore sandals, not shoes and stockings as we do; thus their feet became dusty as they walked about. After the woman had wiped his feet, she began kissing them. Over and over again she kept on kissing Jesus' feet. Can you picture how the people stared as she continued to cry and kiss his feet? Finally she took a bottle of very expensive perfume and poured it over Jesus' feet.

Simon saw all this taking place. He said to himself, If Jesus were really a prophet, He would know what sort of woman this is who is touching and kissing and caressing Him. Jesus knew what Simon was thinking and said to him, "Simon, I have something to say to you."

Simon said, "What is it, Teacher?"

Then Jesus told him this little parable. Two men owed money to a certain moneylender. One owed him five hundred denarii, and the other fifty. Neither of them had the money to pay him back, so he canceled the debts of both. Jesus asked Simon, "Now which of them will love him more?"

Simon replied, "The one, I suppose, to whom he forgave more."

"You have judged rightly," Jesus said. Then He turned to the woman and said to Simon, "Do you see this woman? I entered your house, you gave Me no water for My feet, but she has wet My feet with her tears and wiped them with her hair. You gave Me no kiss, but from the time I came in she has not ceased to kiss My feet. You did not anoint My head with oil, but she has anointed My feet with ointment."

Then He continued with the words of our text: "Therefore I tell you, her sins, which are many, are forgiven, for she loved much; but he who is forgiven little, loves little."

Jesus contrasted the action of Simon with that of the woman in order to teach Simon that those who have many sins forgiven will show much love.

Let us now apply this lesson to ourselves as we consider the theme,

Lots of Love
I. How do we get lots of love?
   A. By being conscious of our sins.
      1. Jesus says, "He who is forgiven little, loves little." If you and I have an imperfect sense of our sins, and if we come seeking only a little forgiveness, the amount of our love will be very small. It is important, therefore, to be aware of lots of sin within us if we are to have lots of love.
      2. The lack of a sense of sinfulness was Simon's problem. He was a Pharisee. We tend to think of Pharisees as "bad guys," but in reality they were very religious people. They were very careful to keep every one of God's commandments. They were even very careful not to associate with the wrong people.
      3. The best way to understand the attitude of the Pharisee is to listen to the story that Jesus told about a Pharisee and a tax collector who went to the temple to pray. (*Retell the story from Luke 18:9-12*). The Pharisees were so scrupulous about keeping all the commandments that they even gave a tenth of the weeds and other plants that grew around their homes or farms.

      The Pharisees wouldn't be caught dead associating with someone who had a bad reputation. You wouldn't ever catch a Pharisee associating with a prostitute. That is why Simon was so shocked that Jesus allowed the woman to touch Him. The Pharisees were very respectable people. Respectability meant always asking, What will the neighbors say if we do this or that? I can just see Simon almost having a fit that this woman came into his house. What is this prostitute doing here? She's going to spoil my dinner party. I wish that horrid creature would get out of here. Then he said to himself, Jesus can't really be a prophet; if He were, He would know what kind of a woman she is and would not allow her to touch or caress Him. That is Simon—Simon pure.

      I don't suppose anyone would catch many members of this congregation associating with a prostitute either—or a bank robber or a rapist or a murderer. Because church members are respectable people, they may be tempted like the Pharisees to feel that they don't want to be contaminated by such people.

4. Now let's consider the woman in the story. This woman of the street knew that she was a sinner. She knew what kind of a life she had led. She was ashamed of it. By her very tears you can see that she had an entirely different attitude about sin than Simon did.

5. The important question is, Where do we see ourselves? Do we stand over here with respectable Simon or over there with that sinful woman as we stand before God? Are we willing to classify ourselves as sinners? Are we willing to say to God, "I'm no better than she is"? Or are we going to classify ourselves with Simon and the other Pharisee in the temple and say, "God I thank you that I'm not like that prostitute"? How different are we in God's sight from the murderers, rapists, and adulterers we read about in the newspaper? How do we see ourselves? Where do we stand? You know, it's a problem for me, too. As a pastor of a church I don't go around killing or raping people. It's very easy for me to think, Oh, I'm not like those people. And I guess the same thing would be true of you, too, wouldn't it?

Before God, would we rather identify with the Pharisees or with the dregs of society? When we come here to church to pray, what is our attitude? Is it "God, I thank you that I'm not like those other people who are sinners, even those members of our congregation who didn't show up today"? Or do we stand in the corner and say, "God be merciful to me, a poor miserable sinner"? If our attitude is like that of Simon and the other Pharisee that Jesus described, we will go out of this church with our sins still clinging to us. If you come to this church service knowing you are a sinner, feeling the weight of sin, shedding bitter tears over those sins, and seeking forgiveness, you will go home forgiven. Jesus said, "Blessed are those who hunger and thirst for righteousness" (Matt. 5:6). This brings us to the other point about how we get lots of love.

B. By taking the forgiveness offered.

1. The mere consciousness of sin is not going to give us lots

of love. You could be extremely conscious of your sinfulness and still not be filled with love. You might be filled with shame or anger, but not with love. You might be angry with yourself, or you might even be angry with God. What needs to take place is that you hear of God's love and take the forgiveness that comes through His love for Christ's sake. God loves you. He wants you. He wants everyone. He wanted this woman, and he wanted Simon. That's why he took the time and trouble to come to Simon's house and to talk to Simon. Remember He said, "Simon, I have something to say to you."

2. God so loved the world that He gave His only-begotten Son. His love worked out the plan of salvation whereby He Himself came to earth to save mankind. Jesus Christ was not a mere human being. He was God in the flesh. God who hates sin came to earth to live among sinners. He allowed human beings to mistreat Him, to persecute Him, to spit in His face, to kill Him. He who hates sin took our sin and clutched it to His breast. He was able to do this because His love for us was greater than His hatred for sin. He came to die in your place and my place. He suffered the consequence of your sin, my sin, the whole world's sin. When God took away your sin, He gave you something in exchange. He gave you Christ's own holiness and perfection. The perfect life that He lived while here on earth is now ascribed to you, and your sins have been laid on Christ. That's the plan of salvation. Once you believe this and put your trust completely in the promise of God's forgiveness because of His love for you and because of what Christ has done, then you begin to be filled with love.

3. The woman in the story not only had a knowledge of her sin and in this way was different from Simon, but she also had heard of God's love for her. Undoubtedly she had heard this from Jesus' own lips. That God would love her so much that she would be forgiven even though she had led such a terrible life—oh, what joy, what a sense of gratitude, what love must have filled and spilled over in her heart! Because she had lots of sin and because that sin was for-

given, she loved much. That's what Jesus was trying to teach Simon in the story about the moneylender.

When you and I bring lots of sin—mountains of sin—to Jesus, and when we take the immense forgiveness for that great pile of sin, we too will be filled with lots of love.

II. How does lots of love express itself?

  A. By being near the object of love.

    1. It is clear that the lack of love on Simon's part led to his indifferent action toward Jesus and to his displeasure at the prostitute's presence and actions. It was not a great love for Jesus based on forgiveness that led Simon to invite Jesus to his house. The fact that he did not go out of his way to show affection proves that. His whole attitude betrays a coolness that developed into displeasure at Jesus' refusal to rebuke the woman.

    2. It was the woman's appreciation for the love of Jesus that forced her to go to a place where she would certainly be scorned and from which she very likely would be expelled. However, nothing could stop her from coming to Jesus. She wanted to be where Jesus was. She needed to be there. It did not matter that all the tongues would wag. She did not care what people would say. She was determined to be with Jesus.

      Undoubtedly, she wanted to hear more gracious words from the lips of Jesus. Undoubtedly, it was to reinforce her faith in the presence of what surely was a hostile group that Jesus turned and addressed her directly.

    3. It is important for us to ask ourselves honestly how much we love Jesus. What do our actions show? It's so easy to think that we love Him very much. This woman loved Jesus and wanted to be where Jesus was, so she came to the house where He was eating. I hope all of you are here today because you want to be here where Jesus is in a special way. The greater your love for Jesus is, the more you want to hear what He has to say to you. A young man who is in love with a girl wants to be with that girl. He wants to spend all of his time with her. That's why young people get married—so that they can be together day and night. If two people love each other very much, but they are sep-

arated and can't see one another, oh, how they long to get a letter from the person they love. They read that letter over and over again. You have received a letter from someone who loves you very much. It's the Bible. How anxious are you to pick it up and read it over and over again? If we have a really great love for Jesus, won't we pick up His letter every day and read it with great joy and eagerness?

B. By demonstrating our love in deeds.

1. Simon did not demonstrate a great love for Jesus. True, he invited Jesus into his house. Jesus was the guest of honor. But Simon did not even offer Jesus the customary greeting kiss or water to wash His feet, nor did he anoint His head with oil. There was no outward expression of love, no expensive gift.

2. The woman, on the other hand, wanted to show her appreciation. Look at her actions. Publicly in front of everyone, she shed tears of repentance and joy. In front of all she wiped His feet with her hair; she kissed His feet! She publicly showed her emotions.

When was the last time we shed tears of joy in church? Are we afraid to show any emotion that displays our love for Jesus? Why? Would we feel shame? Have you ever individually and publicly said, "I love Jesus"? Why not do it now? Turn to the person on either side, in front, and behind you. Say, "I love Jesus!" If tears come to your eyes, don't be ashamed. (*Pastor, pause for them to do it; you leave the pulpit and say it to others.*)

3. (*After entering the pulpit again*) There was one other deed with which the woman demonstrated her love for Jesus. She gave a tangible gift—the expensive perfume that she poured over Jesus' feet. Was it a waste? People very much in love give gifts, often extravagant gifts; the cost doesn't even enter the picture.

How eager are we to bring gifts to God through the church? Love must express itself somehow. If we love Him much, we just need to show that we love Him by giving tangible gifts. Perhaps I have laid a heavy guilt trip on you, probably triggered severe guilt feelings. If so, I want you to know that God loves you very much, even if you don't love

Him very much. Even if you don't love Him at all, He still loves you. Your lack of love is not going to change His love for you.

4. Certain of His love for you, you can bear to hear a serious word from our Lord. Perhaps He would say to us as He did to Simon, "I have something to say to you. Are you willing merely to entertain or patronize Me? You realize, of course, that Simon did not hate Me. He did not persecute Me. In fact, he invited Me to his home. He was willing to take time for Me. He was even willing to spend some money on Me; a party costs money to buy the food and things. Simon's attitude toward Me, however, was entirely different from that of the sinful woman's. Simon could have taken Me or left Me; it wouldn't have made any difference to him. But oh, that woman! How she loved Me because she knew she had many sins, and all of these many sins were forgiven! How is it with you?"

Conclusion

Having heard how we get lots of love, I hope you can say with the hymn writer: "Chief of sinners though I be, Jesus shed his blood for me." Even though you may be the worst sinner in all the world, Jesus died for you! He loves you. Why not say to God today, "God, I am not as good as I think I am. I don't love You as much as I claim to. Be merciful to me, a poor sinful being"? I hope you trust God enough and know His love well enough to bring a whole pile of sins to Him for His forgiveness. Don't be like Simon; be like the woman. Confess your sins to Him. Take His forgiveness and be free. Be free like the woman to express your love and appreciation to Him, free to serve Him with your whole life. May you have lots of love for God.

God Expects Results
John 15:1-5

Text: I am the true Vine, and My Father is the Vinedresser. Every branch of Mine that bears no fruit, He takes away, and every branch that does bear fruit He prunes, that it may bear more fruit. You are already made clean by the Word which I have spoken to you. Abide in Me, and I in you. As the branch cannot bear fruit by itself, unless it abides in the vine, neither can you, unless you abide in Me. I am the Vine, you are the branches. He who abides in Me, and I in him, he it is that bears much fruit, for apart from Me you can do nothing.

Sermon Study

Exegetical Notes

Though some exegetes consider the opening words to be a parable or allegory, the words "I am the *true* Vine" seem to preclude such interpretation. The absence of any particle of comparison and the definite article *hē* with the word *alēthinē* (true, real) indicate that we should not take these words to be a parable or allegory.

Jesus declares that He is the true, the real, the authentic "Vine." Only in Christ can Christians live. Only in Him is there fruitfulness in true service to God.

Reminding us of the Old Testament description of Israel as God's vineyard, these words could also be an allusion to the fact that Old Testament Israel was only a "type" for Christ, that He is the true "planting of God." In addition, the rejection of what Israel had come to be and its replacement by Christ is another lesson to be learned by the disciples as the New Testament era dawns.

However, the whole section stresses the desire of God for fruitfulness on the part of the branches (cf. vv. 2, 4, 7-8, 16). The necessity for believers to bear fruit is therefore the main thrust of these verses.

What are we to understand by the word "fruit"? It is best to equate "fruit" with discipleship.

1. In Scripture "bearing fruit" is a familiar image for living the life of discipleship. Cf. Rom. 7:4-6; 2 Cor. 9:8; Phil. 1:11; Col. 1:10; etc.

In addition consider that the ultimate purpose for Christ's work of redemption was to enable the saved to serve God with deeds.

2. The purpose of Christ's coming was to give "Himself for us to redeem us from all iniquity and to purify for Himself a people of His own who are zealous for good deeds" (Titus 2:14; see also Eph. 2:10).

3. The blood of Jesus Christ not only cleanses us from sin but also purifies our consciences "from dead works to serve the living God" (Heb. 9:14).

Stewardship Application

The essence of stewardship is to make the business that has been entrusted to the steward profitable for the owner. The steward is expected to produce. If he can't manage the resources so that the business prospers, or if through the lack of faithfulness (trustworthiness) he neglects the business so that no profit is produced, the steward will lose his position. Each of the stewardship parables that Jesus told has this emphasis.

This text states clearly why God can expect results from Christian stewards:

1. They are branches in Christ, who provides them with all that is necessary to produce fruit. True, the fruit hangs on the branches, but what makes the production of fruit possible flows from the stem.

2. The Father prunes and trims away what would prevent fruit—abundant fruit—from forming.

There is no excuse as long as the connection to the stem is solid; fruit must result. See also Rom. 8:9-13.

In teaching stewardship truths the pastor must not shy away from stating clearly that God expects a productive life. The branch that bears no fruit is in danger of being cut off and thrown away. See also Luke 13:6-9.

Sermon Outline

Theme: God Expects Results

Brief

I. Because we are in Christ and thus able to bear fruit.

II. Because He cuts off unfruitful branches.

III. Because He prunes branches that do produce.

Detailed

Introduction

Why did Jesus die on the cross and rise again? What does the blood of Jesus do? (*Pause long enough for people to answer.*) Paul wrote to Titus that the purpose of Christ's coming was to "purify for Himself a people of His own who are zealous for good works" (2:14). Surprised? The writer to the Hebrews states that the blood of Jesus cleanses our consciences "from dead works to serve the living God" (9:14). Does that surprise you? To say merely that Christ died to save us, to say that the blood of Jesus cleanses us from all sins and nothing more, distorts the truth.

One day as Jesus was on his way to Jerusalem during the time figs were to be ripe, He saw a leafy fig tree that seemed to promise fruit. When He went over to pick some fruit, there was none. Immediately He cursed the tree so that by the following day it was withered.

Did Jesus actually do such a thing? Some people can't picture Jesus as a demanding person. They find this action of Jesus incongruous with their concept of Him. But you can read about this event for yourself in Mark 11:12-14, 20-21.

Most citizens seem to expect little good to happen from their local or national government agencies. To get by with as little as possible is the attitude of many in school and at work. It seems hardly anyone wants to be held accountable, whether it be the vilest criminal or the respectable housewife, the banker or the production-line worker.

Such an attitude even seems to have permeated the church. Not only are members often upset with a congregation that expects something of them, but some pastors also have sought to deny responsibility for results. I fear the average church member and even some pastors don't believe God is really serious about the stewardship of the mission that He has given His followers. The low priority so many give to worship and church work and to living the kind of life God wants leads me to that conclusion. That the church is satisfied with such a low level of response is perhaps the greatest tragedy. God cannot tolerate lukewarmness! Therefore, let us consider our text under the theme,

God Expects Results

I. Because we are in Christ and thus able to bear fruit.

    A. We are in Christ.

        1. God expects results because we are in Christ. In Him we are able to bear fruit. Jesus tells us that He is the true Vine and we are the branches. As a living branch is connected to the vine, so are we connected to Christ. An apple branch that is connected to the trunk of the tree can produce apples. It is that union between the branch and the tree that makes it possible.

        It is only our union with Christ that makes it possible to produce the results God expects from our lives. Jesus says, "As the branch cannot bear fruit by itself, unless it abides in the vine, neither can you, unless you abide in Me" (John 15:4).

        It is our baptism that unites us with Christ and with His death and resurrection (see Rom. 6:3-11). We abide in Jesus as we continue to trust in Him as the only Savior from sin and eternal damnation.

        2. God made you to be a branch in Christ. Branches don't come into being except as they grow on the trunk. So it is with us and Christ. It was for a very definite purpose that God made us branches in Christ. He did it so that we would be able to bear fruit for Him. The Bible makes these two points in Eph. 2:8, 10: "By grace you have been saved through faith; and this is not your own doing, it is the gift of God. . . . For we are His workmanship, created in Christ Jesus for good works, which God prepared beforehand, that we should walk in them."

        This same truth is clearly expressed in the words of Jesus, "You did not choose Me, but I chose you and appointed you that you should go and bear fruit" (John 15:16). It is solely the action of God that made us branches in Jesus Christ.

The whole purpose of Christ's suffering, dying, and rising again was to give us power to serve God. We were freed from sin so that we could serve God.

B. What happens when we are in Christ?

1. What happens when you are in Christ? Just as a branch receives from the stem or trunk sustenance that makes it possible for the branch to bear fruit, so our life as branches in Christ gives us the nourishment that makes fruit-bearing possible. Christ gives us not only the desire to live for God, but He makes the actual living possible. As branches connected to Christ, we can draw on all the power of God to produce the fruit. Being in Christ makes us new creatures.

2. In a very real sense one could say that it is Christ who produces the fruit through us. Just as in the physical body the head first plans a certain action and then makes the muscles do certain things, so Christ controls and moves those who are in Him. The desire and the actual words and deeds originate and flow from Him, just as the sap that produces the fruit flows from the stem of a vine through the branches. The apostle Paul puts it in these words: "I have been crucified with Christ; it is no longer I who live, but Christ who lives in me; and the life I now live in the flesh I live by faith in the Son of God, who loved me and gave Himself for me" (Gal. 2:20).

Since it doesn't depend on our ability but on the ability that is flowing through us by our connection to Christ, and since Christ therefore is the one who is producing fruit through us, God can and does expect results.

II. Because He cuts off unfruitful branches.

A. A branch that does not bear fruit is cut off.

1. Jesus says in our text, "Every branch of Mine that bears no fruit, He takes away" (John 15:2). God is serious that branches should bear fruit. If He did not expect fruit, He would not cut off unproductive branches. What good is a vine branch that doesn't produce grapes? Just so, what good is a Christian that produces no fruit? Christians are branches in Christ to produce fruit. That is our only purpose for existing.

2. Jesus teaches a similar lesson in Matt. 5:13: "You are the salt of the earth; but if salt has lost its taste, how shall its saltness be restored? It is no longer good for anything except to be thrown out and trodden under foot by men."

In the same way, branches that don't produce are good for nothing; they are cut off and burned. Jesus speaks this strong word of warning, because God is serious. He expects fruit from your life. If not, there would be no reason to cut off branches that did not produce.

Notice that Jesus does not say that the Father cuts off all branches except the best producers. Even though God does not tolerate branches that are totally unfruitful, there is yet hope for the weak producers.

B. Why such severe action?

1. Because the mission that God has entrusted to each one of His followers is so important, He must insist on performance. For the followers of Jesus to be unprofitable stewards who do not pay attention to their task is unthinkable. God has entrusted to Christians the task of bringing the message of His reconciling action in Christ to the world.

2. God wants the world to know, love, and trust in Him. He is deeply involved and has made a considerable investment in securing salvation for the whole world. That salvation cost Him much. At creation He merely said, "Let it be," and there it stood. It was not so with redemption. That was carried out according to a special plan. God got personally involved in the work with His own being. The eternal Son of God came to earth to give His life.

God is not about to let this work fail. There is too much at stake. Since Christians are to be His instruments in continuing this important work, He expects to see fruit. A lukewarm attitude will not do. Thus Jesus says that those who are unwilling to give their all cannot be His disciples. Putting it bluntly, during His earthly ministry Jesus said we must take up our cross and follow Him or forget it.

III. Because He prunes branches that do produce.

A. Pruning is necessary for good results.

    1. It involves cleaning the producing branches. Jesus informs us that every branch in Him that does bear fruit will be pruned so that it produces more. Those not acquainted with the way grapes are produced would be shocked to see a vineyard after the pruning. All unnecessary growth is cut off. Those who want a good harvest prune diligently and carefully.

    2. Just as the part of the branch on a grape vine that does not aid and may even actually hinder the production of more grapes is cut off, so God also prunes our lives of whatever keeps us from producing more. Whatever would distract us from our task must be taken away.

B. Pruning hurts.

    1. Often people do not understand the value of the pruning that God does in their own lives or in the lives of others. When God prunes our life, it hurts. We feel the pain. We may rebel and even become angry with God as He cuts and trims things out of our lives, but He knows what He is doing. It all has a gracious purpose.

    2. The purpose of the pruning is to make your life more useful in Christ. As God takes away that which distracts, we can see our mission in life more clearly. When we ourselves are brought to tears and pain, we can be more useful to others in understanding. When we ourselves learn that only God can help, we grow in our trust and dependence. When we continue to look to God in severe trials, it enables us to explain and demonstrate to others how important God is. Your trust and dependence on Him becomes a powerful example to others. Many of the great hymns of the church were written by those going through severe trials. (*Cite an example that you have found inspiring.*)

Conclusion

Christian stewardship requires using every opportunity to advance God's kingdom. God wants you to succeed. Therefore, He enables you to produce. He engrafted you into Christ. He gives you all you need to succeed in carrying out your stewardship responsibilities.

Why is it that so often we are such poor stewards? Why is it that we seem to produce so little fruit? Is it because we fail to recognize that God expects results? Or is it because we forget that we must depend on Jesus, the true Vine, for strength and try to find it elsewhere? Or is it because we fail to see the good in the Father's pruning in our life and resent it?

Hear the words of your Savior: "You did not choose Me, but I chose you and appointed you that you should go and bear fruit and that your fruit should abide; so that whatever you ask the Father in My name, He may give it to you" (John 15:16). In your work of bearing abundant fruit—in your stewardship responsibility of using your whole life for the sake of the mission of making disciples of the whole world—Jesus promises that whatever you ask the Father in His name, He will give it to you.

There is no excuse for not bearing fruit. All you need is supplied by God. Only willful disobedience or inaction will cause you to be unfruitful. God wants you to succeed. Depend on Him.

Good Stewards
1 Peter 4:10

Text: As each has received a gift, employ it for one another, as good stewards of God's varied grace.

Sermon Study

Exegetical Notes

The word *hekastos* is placed first to receive the main emphasis. "As *each* has received a gift, etc." Each individual has received a gift from the Holy Spirit (see 1 Cor. 7:7; 12:7). The last citation limits *hekastos* to Christians. The manifestations of the Holy Spirit, as the Spirit Himself, are not given to unbelievers.

The words *received, gift,* and *grace* combine to emphasize that the individual cannot take credit for having this ability. Because they are gifts, there is no room for pride or the exalting of one person above the other because of what he is able to do. If anyone is to be praised, it is God.

The Greek *eis heautous* emphasizes that the gifts are not to be used for the personal benefit of the individual but for the church. The words "varied grace" indicate that these gifts are not all the same. What God gives to individuals varies from one person to the next. All the skills and abilities that the church needs are found in the individual members. What one individual cannot do another will be able to do.

A steward is one to whom certain property is entrusted to be administered according to the owner's will or direction. The adjective "good" is a translation of the Greek word *kalos,* which has the flavor of grace and beauty. It describes the manner in which gifts are put to work in the church (see 1 Cor. 13). Had the Greek word *agathos* been used, it would have emphasized moral goodness.

A good steward does not hide or bury the resources or fail to be trustworthy in conducting the master's business (see Matt. 25:14-30). In a loving, gracious manner these individual gifts from God are to be used in such a way as to carry out the master's will faithfully.

Stewardship Application

There can be no quarrel with the Reformation emphasis on the principle of the "priesthood of all believers." The privilege and responsibility of each individual is fully documented in Scripture. The priesthood of all believers declares that each individual has the right—and therefore must assume that he has the ability—to serve the Lord.

The church ought not encourage its members merely to be spectators. It ought to know what gifts each individual has and encourage their use for the benefit of the whole body. As the various parts of the human body function together to make the body effective, just so each member of the congregation needs to contribute his special ability, given by God for the good of all. To limit the stewardship of the member merely to giving money thwarts God's purpose and the intention for which He gave each individual specific gifts.

Christian stewardship is the recognition and fulfillment of a task assigned by God. Inherent in stewardship is also the idea that the steward is responsible and accountable for specific resources that he is to manage in order to accomplish the task assigned.

This text offers the preacher a splendid opportunity to open the door to greater involvement on the part of each member of the congregation. Using his special gift to help others in the congregation not only gives satisfaction but also encourages more enthusiastic participation. But we must be careful not to use this text to coerce or shame people into doing "church work" in an area for which they have not been gifted.

Sermon Outline

Theme: Good Stewards

Brief
  I. Good stewards acknowledge that what they have comes from God.
  II. Good stewards use what has been given them to serve others.

Detailed

Introduction

In 1808 a grand performance of *The Creation* took place in Vienna. Franz Joseph Haydn, the composer, was present, but he was so old and feeble that he had to be wheeled in a chair into the theater. This was the last time that Haydn appeared in public. The presence of the old man aroused intense enthusiasm among the audience that could no longer be suppressed as the chorus and the orchestra burst into full power on the superb passage, "And there was light."

Amid the tumult of the enraptured audience the old composer was seen striving to raise himself. Once on his feet, he mustered up all his strength and in reply to the applause of the audience he cried out as loud as he was able, "No, no! Not from me but," pointing to heaven, "from thence—from heaven above—comes all!" Then he fell back into his chair, faint and exhausted, and had to be carried out of the room (adapted from Basil Miller, *Treasury of Stewardship Illustrations* [Kansas City, Mo: Beacon Hill Press, 1952]. Used by permission of the publisher.).

The very essence of stewardship is to realize that everything comes from God and that we only get to manage what He places in our hands. Though we may often act as if the things we possess belong to us, in reality God has never relinquished His ownership of anything. Good stewards acknowledge this.

On the basis of our text let us consider the theme,

Good Stewards

I. Good stewards acknowledge that what they have comes from God.
   A. Each has received a gift.
      1. Each one of us has received a gift, a special ability from God. Each Christian is singled out as an individual to whom gifts and abilities have been entrusted. Every Christian is included; no one is omitted. Each one has received his particular gift; each has been made a manager over a certain portion of God's possession.
      2. The Christian church is pictured in Scripture as a body. Each of the various parts of our physical bodies has certain special functions to perform. These are tasks that no other part of the body can do. The same is true of believers. They

are parts of the body of Christ. They too have special tasks to perform. There is a special part that each of us has to play in God's scheme of things.

3. Are you aware of your special gift from God? You have one! Sometimes Christians don't consider themselves to be worth much to God. They don't see themselves as playing an important role in His work. Christ died for you. He shed His blood to cleanse you from sin and to fit you for service in His kingdom.

As we see others at work in the congregation, doing things that we don't or can't do, it is easy to say, "I don't count for much in this congregation; I am not important." When that happens, we tend to sit on the sidelines and watch others. God did not intend for this to be your role. Each Christian has been given something special from God.

B. It is a gift.

1. The second point our text makes is that our special ability is a gift; it comes by God's grace. All that we have, no matter what it is—even money—can be traced back to God. If God had not given you certain physical skills such as walking, talking, seeing, and thinking, you could not earn money. Often we forget this and take the credit ourselves for what we have.

2. We didn't determine the build of our bodies or the hundred other features that make us different from every other person. We had nothing to do with the inclination that allows us to become a musician or an artist or an outstanding athlete. All these things were in place at the time of our birth. All we can do is either develop them or let them lie idle.

The apostle Paul reminded the Corinthian congregation: "Who sees anything different in you? What have you that you did not receive? If then you received it, why do you boast as if it were not a gift?" (1 Cor. 4:7).

3. How silly it is to fret over physical features. Sometimes you teenagers are distressed by the shape of your nose, ears, legs, or toes. God made your body the way it is. He made another person's body different. So what? Your body is God's gift for you to use to His glory.

Our text tells us that the gift we have is God's gift to us. The wise God who has a special task for you to do has equipped you especially for that task. Would it not be foolish to say, "Take it back, God. I don't want it. I don't need it"? It is just as foolish to say, "I did it all on my own. Look at what *I* accomplished!"

C. The gift is by grace.

1. As we acknowledge that everything we have comes from God, the question arises, Why? Why did I get this gift or ability and not someone else?

   When we recognize that much of what we have in life had its beginning before we had anything to do with it, we can recognize that it is by grace. It is not what we did or what we were that made God give us this or that particular gift. We had done nothing to deserve it.

   And when we look at what we do with our lives, we must marvel at God's patience, mercy, and grace. Far too often we ignore God's will for our lives. Do you consciously live every moment, say every word, and do every deed so that it all helps accomplish the mission God has given you? Surely not! Are we diligently using the special gifts He has given us for His glory? God's grace is everywhere evident. That we have and continue to have the gifts is due to that grace.

2. Anything that we receive by grace is something that we have not earned. There is no room for anyone's boasting about the gift. There is no room for pride in personal achievement for what we accomplish with the gift. What we are and what we have is from God. Who gets what gift is His decision alone. The Bible says that God distributes to each one individually just as He determines (1 Cor. 12:11).

II. Good stewards use what has been given them to serve others.

A. Serve God first and foremost.

1. We are to serve God Himself first and foremost. We are His stewards. The result of our stewardship is that in everything Jesus Christ may be glorified. The purpose for our lives on earth is to advance God's cause. He is anxious for the world to know Him as a kind and loving Father.

Jesus Christ, through His earthly life, revealed the Father for what He is—the God of love. Through the proper use of our special gifts, each one of us in our own way can continue to reveal our Father as that same loving God. What a glorious privilege, what a high honor has been given to us! We are stewards, true, but more than that, we are also sons and daughters of the most high God!

2. Serving our loving Father means He must come first. Unless He has first place in our lives, He has no place. He cannot play second fiddle to anyone or anything and still be God. His very nature demands that we love Him with all our heart, with all our soul, and with all our mind. "This is the great and first commandment. And a second is like it, You shall love your neighbor as yourself" (Matt. 22:37-39). As forgiven and redeemed children, we put God first, not out of slavish fear but in grateful appreciation for His love in Christ Jesus.

B. We use the gift for one another.

1. We are to use the gifts we have received for one another. God has not given us our gifts for our own enjoyment as private possessions; they are to be used in the congregation. As we serve one another, we serve God.

2. The individual parts of the physical body serve each other so that the body can accomplish its tasks. As members of Christ's body, the church, we must all work together supporting each other. Only if each member contributes his special gift to the work of the whole will the church be efficient. (*Use examples of how each component part of the space shuttle is necessary for a successful operation.*)

C. The gift is intended to be used.

1. The final point that we want to make from our text is that the gifts are intended to be used. The phrase "as good stewards" (as managers) indicates that the gifts still belong to God. We are not the actual owners but merely the stewards of our gifts. As stewards we are in control of their use. As managers, administrators, or executors, we must make the decisions concerning when and how our gifts are used. When we use them for the good of the whole body—to serve one another—we consult with one another. We

cannot use our gifts as God intended if we just use them independently, without regard for the other members.

2. We are to use the gifts we have been given. If we, like the wicked servant of Matt. 25, have kept our gifts buried, we are unprofitable stewards. We stand in danger of losing what we have. If you have been guilty of burying the gift, repent. God will forgive and help you. God is a gracious God, eager to see you succeed in your stewardship.

Conclusion

Brothers and sisters in the Lord, fellow members of His body, you have been specially chosen and picked by God; you have been loved, forgiven, redeemed, made fit for heaven, and given special gifts with which to accomplish His will on earth.

Let us overcome selfishness and the temptation to ignore other people's needs in order to satisfy our desires, both for things and for self-praise. Let us use our own special gifts to help the other parts of the body so that we all can be about our Father's business.

Part 3
SERMONIC BIBLE STUDIES

The regular Bible study classes on Sundays will not reach most of the members of the congregation. A sermonic Bible study is a method by which at least all who are in public worship would be reached.

What Is a Sermonic Bible Study?

A sermonic Bible study replaces the regular sermon. It explains and applies a portion of Scripture verse by verse. Since it is limited to a specific text, it is not as complete as a Bible study that can examine a large number of different passages.

Pastors, these pages are intended for your use. You may want to use them on Sunday morning just as they are, or you can use them as helps to develop your own sermonic Bible studies. The people in the pews should have a printed copy of the Bible section so they may follow and participate.

The Revised Standard Version is used as the basis for the text since most people are using that version. If you use another version, you will have to make adjustments in the material of each study since the specific word references won't match.

Feel free to be innovative and adapt the format to whatever is acceptable in your congregation. This format is not structured to allow for verbal responses from the congregation. If your congregation would be comfortable with open discussion or with one or more individuals making responses that you have planned with them in advance, it might be more interesting.

Before using these sermonic Bible studies, please be very familiar with the entire content. Also, it would be most advantageous to you if you were to practice this with someone so that you could check your timing. Not all of us speak at the same rate of speed.

God bless you as you seek to lead your people into a correct understanding of what stewardship is all about. It is imperative that members have the same grasp of Biblical stewardship that their pastors have.

God's Managers
Luke 16:1-13

Purpose: To understand the word "stewardship" and its ramifications.

Christians ought to wise up. The people of the world have often said this, but so has our Lord Jesus Christ. When the people of the world say it, they mean it in a derogatory sense, but when our Lord says that Christians ought to wise up, He means it in a helpful sense. Though the admonition has been appropriate since the beginning of the church, it has become especially imperative in our day and age that we Christians become good stewards or wise managers of what God has entrusted to us. It is highly desirable, therefore, that we recapture the Biblical concept of *stewardship*.

In order to understand what God expects of us as His stewards, we are going to study a section of Scripture in which the word *stewardship* is used three times. By the way, the Greek word that is translated "stewardship" is only used nine times in the entire New Testament.

(Have the congregation read the text with you either in unison, verse by verse, or by sections. You could read the first six words as introduction. Part of the congregation could read verses 1b-2; another part could read 3-7; another, 8-9; and another, 10-13.)

People have called this parable by various names—the unrighteous steward, the dishonest steward, the shrewd manager, etc. Some even dislike the parable; they find it offensive. It seems as if Jesus is praising dishonesty. As we study these words of our Lord, let us remember that the point of the story is that the people of this world are smarter in their business than Christians are in carrying out God's mission. Let us study these words of Jesus with the purpose of "wising up." For the Spirit will enlighten us through the words we will study. (*Here offer a prayer for the Lord's guidance in the study.*)

Notice that the parable is intended for Jesus' followers. "He also said to the disciples." His words are not intended for the people of the world, the unbelievers. They would not understand them. They are for those who belong to Jesus. Immediately we need to ask, Do these words apply to me? If I have been called by Him to be His follower, to be His own, surely these words do apply to me.

What kind of a follower of Jesus am I? The first 12 that Jesus chose weren't too bright; often they did not understand things correctly. Once when they were afraid in a storm He called them men "of little faith." Even after they had been with Jesus for three years, they didn't understand the crucifixion, nor did they expect Him to rise from the grave. But Jesus didn't give up on them. He even entrusted the continuation of His mission to them. Are we any smarter than those first disciples? Perhaps somewhat—in some ways. But it is surprising how much learning we still have to do. Today perhaps many of us are going to learn some things, even some surprising things. Let's all bow our heads and pray together, "Lord, teach me."

Jesus started His teaching with a story: "There was a rich man who had a steward, and charges were brought to him that this man was wasting his goods." In some translations the word *steward* is translated as *manager*. One translation even uses the word *trustee*. What was the steward's job? If we look at verses 5-7, we see that he managed either revenue-producing land or a business that dealt in farm produce (oil and grain).

Apparently, the owner did not keep close watch on his steward or manager. "Charges were brought to him that this man was wasting his goods." The master did not discover this himself; it was reported to him. The word *goods* is translated as *possessions* or *property* in other versions. The Lord doesn't picture him as stealing. His problem apparently was poor management, probably poor record keeping. People were getting by without paying their bills. Notice in verses 5-7 that the steward even had to ask, "How much do you owe my master?"

Let's read verse 2 together: "And he called him and said to him, 'What is this that I hear about you? Turn in the account of your stewardship, for you can no longer be steward.'" One translation has "your handling of my property" for "your stewardship." That is what stewardship is—the handling or managing of someone else's property.

What do most people think about when they hear the word *stewardship*? If you said, "Money," you are correct. Studies have shown over and over again that the first association people make with *stewardship* is money or budgets. As we see from this particular portion of Scripture, as well as from the use of the word in other places in the Bible, stewardship is really the whole business of managing. Of course, the position of manager requires faithfulness in details. It is the manager's responsibility to see to it that the business prospers or succeeds. The manager or steward must make proper use of the resources. What if God were to require an audit of you today of the performance of your stewardship? Would He say, "Well done, good and faithful servant"? By the way, accountability is a very important feature of our relationship with God. Someday you will want to read Matthew 24 and 25, as well as Luke 12, 16, and 19 to understand this accountability.

Let us now read verses 3 and 4: "And the steward said to himself, 'What shall I do, since my master is taking the stewardship away from me? I am not strong enough to dig, and I am ashamed to beg. I have decided what to do, so that people may receive me into their houses when I am put out of the stewardship.' " The preliminaries of the parable, verses 1 and 2, are brief; the main point, the shrewdness of the steward, is elaborated at length. We are shown his reasoning, his prompt decision, and the instant execution of his shrewd plan. He did not delay; he considered at once what he should do. He had little time. If he could do anything, it had to be done at once. So he asked himself, What is possible under the circumstances? What shall I do? The unjust steward faced reality too late. But when he understood the facts, he did something about the situation. The question is, Do we Christians live in a dream world?

The person of the world cares a great deal about his desires and pleasures, but the followers of Christ are often so casual about their souls and the kingdom of God. The golfer takes lessons and reads books and magazines about golfing, while the church member often forgets his prayers or reads the Bible with little enthusiasm. The salesman becomes an evangelist for some gadget, while the disciple of Jesus rarely mentions the Savior of the world to others. People of the world can sing the praises of certain television programs, while Christians often neglect to say anything about the value of worship and the blessings they receive from their church.

Now let's look at verse 8: "The master commended the dishonest steward for his shrewdness; for the sons of this world are more shrewd in dealing with their own generation than the sons of light." Since it cannot be said with complete certainty whether "master" refers to Jesus or to the master of the steward in the parable, the fact that the master commended the dishonest steward for his shrewdness poses a problem for many people. The point, however, is not that the master or the Lord commended the dishonesty of the steward; he was commending his shrewdness, his prudence. That is exactly what the last half of the verse says: "The sons of this world are more shrewd in dealing with their own generation than the sons of light." Even though the steward lost his position through mismanagement, he planned for an earthly future. The followers of Christ are to look forward to an eternal, heavenly destiny. Most people believe in savings accounts, pension plans, IRAs, insurance, and other investments as preparations for their future in this world. But what preparations are we making for our eternal home? How much attention do we pay to the words of Jesus, "Do not lay up for yourselves treasures on earth, where moth and rust consume and where thieves break in and steal, but lay up for yourselves treasures in heaven, where neither moth nor rust consumes and where thieves do not break in and steal" (Matt. 6:19-20).

Let's read verses 10-13 together: "He who is faithful in a very little is faithful also in much; and he who is dishonest in a very little is dishonest also in much. If then you have not been faithful in the unrighteous mammon, who will entrust to you the true riches? And if you have not been faithful in that which is another's, who will give you that which is your own? No servant can serve two masters; for either he will hate the one and love the other, or he will be devoted to one and despise the other. You cannot serve God and mammon."

The steward in the parable was discharged because he was not a good manager. He was not faithful in attending to his master's business. He let other concerns occupy his time. He didn't even know how much people owed his master. Faithfulness is the point of this last section. The question that you and I and all Christians need to ask ourselves is, Are we living for our Master? Are we living to serve God? Or are we merely living for worldly things? The point that Jesus makes in verse 13 is that you cannot serve both.

God has prepared eternal salvation for us. Christ has earned the right for us to be in heaven. The Holy Spirit has given us faith and trust in the Savior Jesus Christ through the Word of the Gospel. In the same grace and mercy He has committed into our hands the important task of bringing the message of Christ's work of salvation to each generation. He has entrusted a very important task to us, something that cost Him dearly. He has given us all the resources necessary to carry out the task that He has assigned to us. He asks that we be good and faithful stewards in carrying out this task.

The question is, How are we managing this work? How careful are we to use what God has given us in order not to lose the great gifts? How eager are we to be good stewards? Our Lord tells us in the last verses of this parable that we cannot serve two masters. Our own human natures and the world make very heavy demands on us. They want us to give all of our time and effort to worldly things. Our old human nature wants us to be concerned about things that bring it pleasure. But God also demands absolute loyalty. We cannot serve or be loyal to both. The Lord would teach us by this parable to be wise and prudent in order that we might be good stewards and not lose our stewardship and all God's other blessings through carelessness. Our Lord tells us not to be concerned about earthly things but to make our first concern the seeking of the kingdom of God and His righteousness.

STUDY 2
Using God's Possessions
Nehemiah 9:6, 15, 21, 24; 10:35

Purpose: To remind ourselves that we are not owners but merely
stewards of God's possessions.

> You arrived in this world without anything, and it is equally
> certain you will take nothing with you when you leave it.
> Not a thing that men call their own actually belongs to them.

Human beings tend to forget God—especially when things are
going well. Even in times of trouble they sometimes live and act as if
God were not involved in this world. We Christians, too, sometimes
forget God in our use of the natural resources of this world. We also
forget when we worry. We don't remember that God is in control. We
need to remind ourselves that even the plans and the schemes of men
are under God's control. The prophet Jeremiah confessed: "I know, O
Lord, that the way of man is not in himself, that it is not in man who
walks to direct his steps" (10:23).

One of the fundamental aspects of Christian stewardship is to
recognize that everything belongs to the Lord. We only get to use and
manage them for God. Everything that man enjoys and possesses comes
to him as the result of the mercy of God. God reveals His love in the
abundant provision He has made for man's needs. Since all that man
has belongs to God, he is a steward, accountable to his Master for the
use he makes of every blessing.

This morning we would like to use five verses out of Nehemiah 9
and 10 to impress on ourselves that everything, including man, belongs
to God through creation and daily preservation. Therefore in thanksgiving we are to be careful stewards of His possessions and not act as

if God were out of the picture and we were complete masters of our own destiny and of all we call our own possessions.

This section of Nehemiah is a hymn of praise to God with the acknowledgment that God, the Creator of heaven and earth, chose Abraham and made a covenant with him to give the land of Canaan to his seed and then that God had in fact kept His promise. It recounts how God delivered His people Israel by great signs and wonders from the power of Pharaoh when He saw their affliction, gave them laws and guidance from Sinai, miraculously provided them with food and water in the wilderness, and made it possible for them to take possession of the Promised Land. Although their fathers rebelled against Him, even in the wilderness God did not withhold His mercy from them but sustained them 40 years so that they lacked nothing. When they turned their backs on Him and worshiped false gods, He chastened them. And when in repentance they came crying to Him for help, He forgave them and restored them again. For His gracious actions they in turn obligated themselves to worship Him with material resources.

As they did this, they acknowledged and reminded themselves that everything comes from the Lord and is really His.

(Here insert a prayer for the Lord's guidance in the study.)

Let us now read the sixth verse of chapter 9: "Thou art the Lord, Thou alone; Thou hast made heaven, the heaven of heavens, with all their host, the earth and all that is on it, the seas and all that is in them; and Thou preservest all of them; and the host of heaven worships Thee."

That God has created all things is a recurrent theme in the whole Bible. This verse says that God has created the heavens, the earth, and the seas. Because He made it, it is all His. Isn't it foolish to think and act as if these things belong to us and God has nothing to say about how they are used?

Not only did God make heaven and earth and the seas, but He also made everything that is in these spheres. "Thou hast made heaven, the heaven of heavens, with all their host." The "host" has been variously understood as stars or angels. In this study we will not concern ourselves with the precise interpretation of the word. All that is on earth—people, animals, plants, minerals, etc.—belongs to Him. God made the seas and all that is in them. All the fish, the crustaceans, the mammals, you name it—whatever is in the sea belongs to God.

This verse also says that God gives life to them all. Not only did God make them; He also keeps them alive. He does this first by His creative Word. The very continued existence of all things depends on God. He placed the life force in each one of them. He continues to sustain them by the food that He gives to them. The psalmist acknowledges this when he says, "Thou openest Thy hand, Thou satisfiest the desire of every living thing" (Ps. 145:16).

Sometimes God does this sustaining in very ordinary ways, and sometimes He does it in very unusual ways. Verses 15 and 21 show God's providing for His people in an extraordinary manner. Let us read these verses together: "Thou didst give them bread from heaven for their hunger and bring forth water for them from the rock for their thirst." Now verse 21: "Forty years didst Thou sustain them in the wilderness, and they lacked nothing; their clothes did not wear out and their feet did not swell." It takes no more effort on God's part to provide bread from heaven (the manna) or to make water flow from a rock, than it does to put the force into seeds that causes them to sprout and grow and produce fruit. Just because God does it so often with seeds, we should not forget that this in itself is a miracle.

When we read that for 40 years their clothing didn't wear out as they traveled through the wilderness, we are astounded. Ordinarily under such circumstances the clothes would soon be torn, and the shoes or sandals would be worn out. These facts remind us again that everything is under God's control. If He so chooses, He can make things last far beyond their normal range. Since the clothes really belong to God, they are subject to His control and desires. That raises the question, How often do we consider the clothes we wear, the automobiles we drive, or the houses we live in as belonging to God?

God's ownership extends far beyond mere physical things. He is in control of the outcome of the schemes and plans of men as well as of their eternal destiny. Look at the last part of verse 15: "Thou didst tell them to go in to possess the land which Thou hadst sworn to give them." Then, as we see from verse 24, He did this by subduing the inhabitants of the land and giving into their hands the kings and the people of the land. Not only are individuals to look to God for guidance and direction for their lives, but nations should also look to God since He controls their destiny. A nation that puts its trust in the Lord is truly blessed. But the nation that puts its trust in alliances or military power and forgets to put its trust in the Lord will soon discover to its dismay that the course of history does not really depend on human might but on what God has in store.

When the apostle Paul revealed the true God at Athens, He said, "What therefore you worship as unknown, this I proclaim to you. The God who made the world and everything in it, being Lord of heaven and earth, does not live in shrines made by man, nor is He served by human hands, as though He needed anything, since He Himself gives to all men life and breath and everything. And He made from one every nation of men to live on all the face of the earth, having determined allotted periods and the boundaries of their habitation" (Acts 17:23-26).

As we live our lives on earth, proper stewardship requires that we worship and bless God remembering that (1) He is our Creator; (2) He is our divine Preserver and Sustainer; and (3) He is guiding and continually ordering our steps.

Isn't it easier to use the things that God has placed at our disposal correctly when we know that everything is His? It is so much easier for us to share with others in their need when we know that what we share isn't really ours; it belongs to God. We are to use His possessions in ways that glorify Him and accomplish His purpose. The children of Israel reviewed the past so that the duty and wisdom of serving God might be impressed on their hearts. As they contemplated God's ownership of all things and God's provision for them, they were led to place themselves willingly under obligation. Let us read the account of that obligation in 10:35: "We obligate ourselves to bring the first fruits of our ground and the first fruits of all fruit of every tree, year by year, to the house of the Lord." They went on to say that they would bring "the first of our coarse meal, and our contributions, the fruit of every tree, the wine and the oil" (v. 37).

When God had taken His people out of Egypt to establish them as a nation, He had commanded them to bring one-tenth of the increase to Him. This action of bringing the first fruits, 10 percent of the yield, to the Lord was to remind the people that everything they had came to them from His gracious and bountiful goodness. The situation of the people in our Bible study is the return of the Israelites from captivity in Babylon. As they reviewed what the Lord had done for them as a nation, they laid this obligation on themselves as a response of faith.

If we consecrate ourselves to the Lord, we need to be aware that this includes the consecration of everything that we call ours. Therefore, all of us need to ask the question, Have I accepted the proposition that I am living primarily for the glory of God, that everything I am and have is His? Do I believe that my heavenly Father is entrusting me with responsibilities and abilities to be administered as a faithful steward of heaven? If I say yes to these questions, do I use His possessions in such a way that His kingdom is profited by my use? Do people come to see and understand God better because of the use I make of what He has entrusted to me?

There is and always will be a big difference between the Christian and the non-Christian. Their attitudes about the use of God's possessions are as different as their eternal destination. Let us beware that the non-Christian, because of their number and influence, don't squeeze us into their mold.

True Christians recognize God not only as the Source but also as the End of life. We recognize that the divine purpose in the creation of man includes a plan and program for each individual life. We realize that God has not placed us into this world to lead a purposeless existence, but that our lives are to fit into the great plan that God is carrying out in regard to the world. We know that the divine purpose for our lives is shaped by infinite knowledge, wisdom, goodness, and love, and that living out of God's purpose offers us the fullest and most satisfying life that is possible.

Freed from Sin
Romans 6:1-14

Purpose: To relate stewardship with justification.

Note to Pastors

This Sunday and next we will study the sixth chapter of the Epistle to the Romans. The material deals with how the one who through faith is righteous shall live. This chapter divides naturally into two parts, based on Paul's beginning each part with the same question. In verse 1: "What shall we say then? Are we to continue in sin that grace may abound?" In verse 15: "What then? Are we to sin because we are not under Law but under grace?" In the first part, verses 1-14, Paul shows that through Baptism we have been incorporated into Christ and thereby are set free from the dominion of sin. In the second part, verses 15-23, he shows that this freedom from sin has been given to us so that we may hereafter serve righteousness. In our Bible study we will consider justification this Sunday and sanctification next Sunday. The first section of Romans 6 deals primarily with justification, and the second deals with sanctification.

Freed from Sin Through Union with Christ

What a superamazing way in which the holy, just God provided salvation for mankind!

God Himself pays for our sin! Christ is punished. We are declared righteous!

God's love is so great that nothing can supersede His grace!

God has His apostle tell us in Romans 8: "Neither death, nor life, nor angels, nor principalities, nor things present, nor things to come, nor powers, nor height, nor depth, nor anything else in all creation, will be able to separate us from the love of God in Christ Jesus our Lord" (vv. 38-39).

Wow! What love! (*Note to pastors: Read this with much excitement and enthusiasm.*)

In His mercy, for Christ's sake, God has declared the unrighteous to be righteous. That is His judgment also on you. No one can contradict it, not even your own conscience. In Romans 5:20 the apostle says, "Where sin increased, grace abounded all the more." So amazing is this grace that people find it hard to believe. Therefore, Paul begins with a question.

Let's read the question: "What shall we say then? Are we to continue in sin that grace may abound?" The thought behind this question is that salvation cannot be that free. The very fact that the objection is raised tells us how explicitly and unreservedly the apostle proclaimed the message of grace. Even people within the church find it difficult to accept justification by faith—by faith *alone*. Recent studies conducted among Lutherans indicate that even within the Lutheran Church many people believe that you have to add something to faith—your works or your good intentions. That should not surprise us because Paul dealt with that same thing in his day. He is speaking to believers who do serious thinking about the blessed truth. He writes, "What shall *we* say then? Are *we* to continue in sin that grace may abound? . . . How can *we* who died . . ." The full acceptance of "the ungodly" by the eternal judge without demanding any merit or worthiness from us is so contrary to everything we consider as fair that we have to be reminded of that truth over and over again.

In this letter the apostle has stated: "No human being will be justified in His sight by the works of the Law" (3:20). And again, "A man is justified by faith apart from works of Law" (3:28). Just prior to our text we read, "Law came in, to increase the trespass; but where sin increased, grace abounded all the more." That we could be declared just, acceptable to God, regardless of any commendatory conduct on our part—such a Gospel was no doubt liable to be mistaken and misrepresented. But notice that the apostle makes no modification.

Paul is not advocating what some have called "cheap grace," however. Let's read verses 2-4: "By no means! How can we who died to sin still live in it? Do you not know that all of us who have been baptized into Christ Jesus were baptized into His death? We were buried therefore with Him by Baptism into death, so that as Christ was raised from the dead by the glory of the Father, we too might walk in newness of life."

Did you notice that in the simplest and most practical terms the apostle makes clear that our justification is not the end of God's plan for us? We have received the "not guilty" verdict not so that we may now walk away from God but that we may walk *with* Him. Because we are justified, we are to be holy, separate from sin. How can we who died to sin still live in it? You and I need to ask this question of ourselves each day.

By our baptism we have been incorporated into Christ. His death is our death, and His resurrection is our resurrection. By virtue of our baptism the benefits of His death and resurrection, as well as the purpose of His death and resurrection, are ours. What a glorious gift is our baptism!

The stewardship of life, the "walking in the newness of life," is not done to earn God's love and favor. The Bible is very explicit on this point. Paul tells us that "while we were yet sinners," that is, before we were converted, "Christ died for us" (Rom. 5:8). Our justification is based on what Christ as our Substitute did in our place. He became our Substitute, our Savior, in order that in thankfulness for having been declared just we might desire to walk in the newness of life. It is out of justification that sanctification proceeds. In the cause-effect relationship, justification is the cause of our sanctification; sanctification is not the cause of our justification. We are declared righteous for Christ's sake.

Let's read verse 5 together: "For if we have been united with Him in a death like His, we shall certainly be united with Him in a resurrection like His." In other places this concept is called "putting on Christ" or "being in Christ." This verse emphasizes that being united with Him in His death (the fact that He has died for us) also means that we are united with Him in His resurrection. His resurrection (the life He now lives) points to the kind of life we should be living.

Let us now read verses 6-11 to amplify what has happened to us through our intimate connection with Christ's death: "We know that our old self was crucified with Him so that the sinful body might be destroyed, and we might no longer be enslaved to sin. For he who has died is freed from sin. But if we have died with Christ, we believe that we shall also live with Him. For we know that Christ being raised from the dead will never die again; death no longer has dominion over Him. The death He died, He died to sin, once for all, but the life He lives He lives to God. So you also must consider yourselves dead to sin and alive to God in Christ Jesus."

What verse 6 describes is, of course, only possible through our baptism. Baptism nails our sinful nature on Christ's cross in order that it might perish in and with the sins for which He died on that cross. A better translation than "sinful body" might be "body of sin," that is, a body that was sold in slavery to sin.

If one individual is sold in slavery to another, when he dies, he is no longer bound to obey his master. That is emphasized so clearly in verse 7: "He who has died is freed from sin." If you have died to sin, you are freed from sin. These statements are still in reaction to the question at the beginning, "Are we to continue in sin that grace may abound?" Isn't it foolish to even ask such a question?(*You may want to develop this verse using "freed" in the forensic sense. Dedikaiōtai literally means "is justified." The sentence literally reads, "He that hath died is justified from sin."*)

The certainty of being dead to sin is also brought out in verses 9-10: "We know that Christ being raised from the dead will never die again; death no longer has dominion over Him. The death He died He died to sin, once for all." Christ will never have to die again for the sins of the whole world. This has been accomplished once and for all, and because Christ was put to death for our sins—in our stead as our Substitute—the benefits of His death accrue to us. Sin and death have no more dominion over us. They can no longer claim us. True, we must still die, but that is not a victory for death. In fact, it becomes our victory. Death has become the way through which we enter into eternal life.

All of this happens in Christ; in Him the verdict of acquittal has been rendered. We are free—free from sin, from death, and from the power of the devil. We are no longer slaves to these. When Christ died, we also in reality died to sin and its power. Death no longer has a hold over us, for Christ who was dead is alive. Remember verse 5: "If we have been united with Him in a death like His, we shall certainly be united with Him in a resurrection like His." And so in verse 11 we are told, "You must also consider yourselves dead to sin and alive to God in Christ Jesus."

Once again, we need to remind ourselves that all of this has happened outside of us. Christ is the one who accomplished all of it. You and I get the benefits by virtue of our baptism, which connects us with Christ—with His death and with His resurrection. When Christ assumed our sins, He made Himself subject to death, which is the penalty for those sins, and so He died for us on the cross. By His death, He expiated all the guilt of our sins. When He died for our sins, He died to sin. He was done with it—and so are we.

Sin, however, still wants our bodily members in order to misuse them for wicked deeds. Therefore, we find a warning in verses 12-14. Let's read them together: "Let not sin therefore reign in your mortal bodies, to make you obey their passions. Do not yield your members to sin as instruments of wickedness, but yield yourselves to God as men who have been brought from death to life, and your members to God as instruments of righteousness. For sin will have no dominion over you, since you are not under Law but under grace." Before our conversion we were dead to God, not able to do His will. As the apostle writes to the Ephesians: "You He made alive, when you were dead through the trespasses and sin in which you once walked. . . . But God, who is rich in mercy, out of the great love with which He loved us, even when we were dead through our trespasses, made us alive together with Christ" (2:1-2, 4-5).

The Law with its demands only increases sin because we cannot obey it perfectly. But we are under grace, not under the Law. Grace simply says, "Hey! You are welcome to come into heaven! Christ has kept all of the demands of the Law for you in your stead, and He has paid the penalty for your disobedience. You are free." It is not demanded of us that we lead a good and holy and perfect life in order to be saved. Christ has already done this for us. If we are dead now to that law of sin, no longer bound to obey it, then in thanksgiving for having been set free from it, we surely don't want to crawl back under it again. Therefore, the stewardship life is not lived as a life of obedience to the Law but as a life of thanksgiving to God, a life lived in appreciation for what God has done for us in justifying us through Christ.

Freed to Serve
Romans 6:15-23

Purpose: To urge living a life of sanctification—living to serve God as good stewards.

The section from Romans 6 that we want to study today might be entitled

Freed from Sin to Serve Righteousness

Last Sunday we ended with verse 14: "You are not under Law but under grace." On the one hand, there is a strong inclination to think that grace alone is insufficient to keep us from sinning. On the other hand, some are inclined to think that since grace pardons sin so freely, one need not be so careful about not sinning. Bitter must have been the pain of the apostle to see this holy freedom distorted into an unholy permission to sin. But he steadfastly refused to alter the teaching that we are saved apart from the deeds of the Law.

How do you handle this freedom? What is your attitude toward the statement that we are not under Law but under grace?

(Here insert a prayer for the Lord's guidance in the study.)

Let us read verse 15 together: "What then? Are we to sin because we are not under Law but under grace? By no means!" At first glance the question seems superfluous to us. But the apostle knows how difficult it is to bring people to understand a consistent preaching of grace, especially to keep them from drawing false conclusions from it. The Law has the effect that when we sin we do so with a bad conscience. But when we are no longer under the Law, there is no longer anyone to condemn us. So why should we be concerned about the kind of life we lead? Or we might be tempted to think that if we sin, we stand under grace anyway and always have access to God's forgiveness. So why should we be so careful about how we live? But is that really what comes of the beautiful teaching of grace? Can the fact that Christians are free from the Law lead them to take sin less seriously?

Church history reveals many perversions of this wonderful teaching of salvation by grace without the deeds of the Law. So the apostle points to the fact that we are free from sin *in order* to serve righteousness. Since we still have the old Adam in us, an empty, unqualified freedom gives sin its best chance to get us under its dominion again. Recall the words of Jesus: "When the unclean spirit has gone out of a man, he passes through waterless places seeking rest, but he finds none. Then he says, 'I will return to my house from which I came.' And when he comes he finds it empty, swept, and put in order. Then he goes and brings with him seven other spirits more evil than himself, and they enter and dwell there; and the last state of that man becomes worse than the first" (Matt. 12:43-45).

Let us now look at verse 16. We read it together: "Do you not know that if you yield yourselves to anyone as obedient slaves, you are slaves of the one whom you obey, either of sin, which leads to death, or of obedience, which leads to righteousness?" Here we have the reason for not living in sin: We become slaves to the one whom we keep obeying.

For a Christian there are only two choices. Either we are going to obey sin, or we are going to obey God. There is no middle ground. Paul is not writing to the unconverted who were never freed from sin; they are involuntary slaves. He is speaking to Christians who by Baptism died to sin and were set free to live to God. Before conversion we do not have a free will. We are slaves to our corrupt human nature. After conversion, having received a new will (spirit), we have a choice. But we don't always make the right choice, do we?

There is a constant battle going on inside us Christians—one force pulling us one way and another force pulling the other way. We must know that if we yield ourselves as slaves to sin, it will lead to death. On the other hand, if we yield ourselves in obedience to God, this will lead to righteousness and a gracious reward in heaven. The word *obedience* in this verse indicates that we have been placed under God. That is whom we are to obey. To obey sin would be disobedience. And conversely, if we were yet under sin, then doing what sin wants us to do would be obedience, and serving God would be disobedience.

How unfortunate it is that some who have been freed to serve God think that grace allows them to commit "little sins" on occasion. True, they do not want to be under the old tyrant, sin, but they think they can indulge in some measure of sin without danger. We all need the reminder of this verse that the one to whom we yield ourselves is the one to whom we become slaves.

Now let's read verses 17 and 18: "But thanks be to God, that you who were once slaves of sin have become obedient from the heart to the standard of teaching to which you were committed, and, having been set free from sin, have become slaves of righteousness." The words "have become obedient" repeat that idea for the fourth time.

The whole Christian life is one of service and obedience; however, it is a willing obedience and service. In chapter 12 the apostle writes: "I appeal to you therefore, brethren, by the mercies of God, to present your bodies as a living sacrifice, holy and acceptable to God, which is your spiritual worship" (v. 1). What a rejoicing there should be in our hearts! We were once slaves of sin, which led to death, but we have been freed from that slavery so that we are now able to serve God.

The words "become obedient from the heart" indicate the sincerity and the depth of this new allegiance that we have willingly given to God. What a change has taken place in the life of one who has become a Christian!

The sinner thinks himself free when he is a slave to sin. But the reality is that he is not free. It is true that while we were sinners, we had to be converted, that is, brought against our will, to this position where we now serve God. But now that we have this commitment to God, we can only say thanks. We have been set free, "emancipated," from the sin. Sin's power is really a usurped authority over us. It stole us from the God who created us and made us into its slaves. When God created the human race, He did not create us to sin. Christians have been freed from that alien power at last so that we now can fulfill the purpose of our being. We are free to obey our Creator and Savior in newness of life.

It may sound strange to call this freedom an enslavement: "slaves of righteousness." If, however, we are on God's side, our true place is with Him. His will is our will. The phrase shows how completely we are now to serve God and to avoid what we once were when we belonged to sin.

Let us now read verse 19: "I am speaking in human terms, because of your natural limitations. For just as you once yielded your members to impurity and to greater and greater iniquity, so now yield your members to righteousness for sanctification." Here the apostle explains why he is using such strong language. Christians, like many adolescents, often find it difficult to handle liberty. Remember the question that was proposed at the beginning of this lesson? Because of our natural limitations, the apostle speaks in terms of complete slavery either to sin or to God. These words remind us of what we read last week from verse 13: "Do not yield your members to sin as instruments of wickedness, but yield yourselves to God as men who have been brought from death to life, and your members to God as instruments of righteousness." There must be a conscious effort on the part of the Christian—with constant prayer—to yield our members to sanctification rather than to sin.

We surely need to pray daily the prayer of the hymn "Take My Life" by Frances R. Havergal. (*Here either read the words of the hymn—* TLH *400;* LW *404*— or ask the congregation to sing it.)

Now let's read the last four verses of the chapter: "When you were slaves of sin, you were free in regard to righteousness. But then what return did you get from the things of which you are now ashamed? The end of those things is death. But now that you have been set free from sin and have become slaves of God, the return you get is sanctification and its end, eternal life. For the wages of sin is death, but the free gift of God is eternal life in Christ Jesus our Lord." Notice the passive verbs in verse 22: "You have been set free from sin and have become slaves of God." Our present state was produced solely by God. We were not able to set ourselves free from sin, neither could we decide for God. God Himself has done these things for us and in us. Now that He has done this for us, we are to serve Him.

Finally, look again at the last verse: "The wages of sin is death, but the free gift of God is eternal life in Christ Jesus our Lord." Each servitude reaches a goal when it is finished. In this respect the two are alike. Yet there is a vast difference between their goals. One pays what is owed—death. The other gives a gift, something not earned—eternal life.

We close this Bible study with the words of our Lord from John 15:5-6: "I am the Vine, you are the branches. He who abides in Me, and I in him, he it is that bears much fruit, for apart from Me you can do nothing. If a man does not abide in Me, he is cast forth as a branch and withers; and the branches are gathered, thrown into the fire and burned." Only as we remain in Jesus Christ, that is, remain connected to Him, are we able to live the life of sanctification—to serve God rather than to serve sin.

PART 4
A LIFE ALIVE UNTO GOD:
Stewardship Bible Study on
1 Corinthians 6:19-20

Paul's original intent in writing these two verses was to help the Corinthians realize that their bodies were not to be used for immoral purposes. However, there is a wider application that can be made of this truth—that we Christians belong to God with all that we are and have.

Your Body Is God's Property

Not only are its physical parts not your own.

Your heart (desires) is not your own.

Your thoughts are not your own.

Your time is not your own.

Your abilities are not your own.

Neither are your material possessions your own, for it was "God's property" that produced them.

A life alive unto God is one that belongs to God because He has bought it for His own and enabled it to serve Him to His glory.

A Life Alive unto God

I. It is a life that belongs to God.
II. It is a life purchased by God to be His.
III. It is a life that has been enabled to serve Him.
IV. It is a life dedicated to living to His glory.

A Life That Belongs to God

You are not Your Own

Some people say life is boring. Others ask, "What is the use of living?" Still others say, "What is the sense of it all?" Perhaps even you yourself have felt like this at times.

On the other hand, some people consider life worthwhile. They wish they could live forever. They wouldn't want it any other way. Such people are full of plans for all the things they hope to accomplish in this life. For them life is exciting.

Many young people ask, "What shall I do with my life?" Sometimes older people ask, "What have I done with my life?" In reality can a Christian ask, "What shall I do with my life?"

In this session we want to examine the stewardship implications raised by the question, Whose life is it? The words from 1 Cor. 6:19, "You are not your own," will direct our Bible study.

1. To whom do the words, "You are not your own," apply? Before answering, read 1 Cor. 6:19-20 and answer a and b.
   a. According to verse 19, why are we not our own?
   b. What additional reason is given in verse 20?
2. Do these verses apply to you personally? For what reasons could you apply them to yourself?
3. According to 1 John 3:8, when and how does it happen that a person belongs to the devil instead of to God?
4. Look also at 1 John 3:10. According to this passage, how can you tell who is a child of God and who is a child of the devil?
5. Why did Jesus call the apostle Peter "Satan" or the devil in Matt. 16:23?

Let's turn our attention now to the spirit and influence of the human life-style that the Bible calls "the world." Read James 4:4 and also 1 John 2:15-17.

6. Is it possible to live for this world and still be a child of God?
7. According to the words of Christ in John 15:18, what is the world's attitude toward Christ?
8. Rom. 12:2 warns us not to be conformed to the world. How does one conform to the world?
9. What happened to Demas (2 Tim. 4:10)?
10. How can a Christian tell if such conformity and love is beginning to affect his life?

There is one other problem area that affects our relationship to God. This is our sinful flesh, sometimes called the old Adam.

11. Read Rom. 8:5-7. According to verse 7, in what relationship to God does the sinful flesh stand?
12. According to verse 6 where does following the dictates of the flesh lead?
13. According to Ps. 51:5, how long has the sinful flesh affected us?
14. According to Galatians 5:24, what do those who belong to God do to the flesh?

It is no wonder that Martin Luther, in his explanation to the sixth petition of the Lord's Prayer, lumps all three of these together as dangerous. He says, "We pray in this petition that God would guard and keep us, so that the devil, the world, and our flesh may not deceive us nor seduce us into misbelief, despair, and other great shame and vice."

15. When 1 Cor. 6:19-20 indicates that you belong to God, what value does that place on your life?
16. What part of life is excluded from God's claim on us?
17. List some of the things included in this claim. (*Ask each member of the class to name at least one.*)
18. Since we don't even belong to ourselves, who has the right to determine what will be done with our life, what our words and actions should be?
19. What do you think the average person in America considers to be the aim and purpose for his life?
20. What do you consider to be the purpose for your life?
21. How does such purpose compare with the priority Jesus sets for us in Matt. 6:33?

22. How does the attitude of the average person in America affect a Christian living in this society?

23. How can you tell if such an attitude has begun to affect your own life and that of your family? (*Give each person a minute to write the answer—then allow them to share their answers with the whole class.*)

24. Remembering what God's Word says about those loving the world and living according to the flesh's desires, what could you, according to justice, expect from God?

25. What do we call that rebellious attitude and those deeds that work at cross-purposes with what God expects of us?

26. According to 2 Cor. 5:21, what did God do with our sins?

27. Because of God's love and for the sake of what Jesus has done for us, when we seek relief from sin, of what does God's Word in 1 John 1:9 assure us?

28. How does 2 Cor. 5:17 describe our condition when we have been brought to look to Christ for forgiveness and life?

29. Although Jesus in Matt. 16 called Peter "Satan," what was He doing for him according to Luke 22:31-32?

30. According to 1 John 2:1-2, what is Jesus doing for you?

31. What has happened to your sin?

32. According to 2 Cor. 5:21, what have we become in Christ?

33. When we realize what we justly deserve and then see what wonderful things God has done for us in Christ, what kind of an attitude develops in our heart?

34. How does this attitude help us live a life alive unto God?

Martin Luther described the life of a Christian as being at one and the same time saint and sinner. As time permits share with one another what this expression means to you.

As far as God is concerned there can be no doubt about it—you are the Lord's. You belong to God. You are His dear child. He has called you by your name, you are His. What is your response to the truth contained in today's lesson? What have you determined to do this week?

SESSION 2
A Life Purchased by God to Be His
Bought with a Price

If you entered a store and made two purchases, one for 50 cents and the other for $5,000, do we need to ask which item you would care for and protect more diligently? Even a child could tell us which purchase would be more precious.

In this lesson we look at our relationship to God in the light of the price He paid for us. Of special interest will be the significance that this costly purchase has for the life we live as stewards.

Martin Luther has captured the heart of today's lesson in his explanation of the Second Article of the Apostles' Creed:

> I believe in Jesus Christ . . . who has redeemed me, a lost and condemned creature, purchased and won me from all sins, from death, and from the power of the devil; not with gold or silver, but with His holy, precious blood and with His innocent suffering and death, that I may be His own, and live under Him in His kingdom, and serve Him . . .

The first words of 1 Cor. 6:20, "you were bought with a price," will give direction to our study today.

1. The first question that comes to mind is, Why was it necessary for God to buy me? A look at Rom. 7:14 gives us one answer. Who is here represented as our owner?
2. According to this passage, what controls the life of the individual?
3. What does Rom. 6:20 call the unconverted?
4. What institution of human interaction is used to picture the condition in which we find ourselves by nature?

5. What is mankind's condition in relationship to God while in the state of being a slave to sin (see Gal. 3:13)?

6. What term does 1 Cor. 6:20 use to describe what brought about the changed condition of the Christian?

7. Who has become the Christian's master?

8. What does Rom. 6:22 call those who have been bought by God?

9. What does Gal. 3:13 call this action of buying us?

10. According to 1 Peter 1:19, what was the price that Christ paid for you? (If you are using the *Good News Bible*—TEV—be aware that it avoids using the word *blood* here, although it is in the original language of the New Testament. Compare also Rom. 3:25 and 5:9 where the word *blood* is also not used by the TEV.)

11. Would you say that was a high price for God to pay? Remembering the introduction to this study,

   a. What does this tell you about the value God places on you?

   b. What does it say about the misuse of your life?

As we are conscious of our faults and failings, we might be tempted to think, Maybe God has changed His mind about me. Maybe He will say, "I made a mistake. It just didn't work out."

Was God's purchase a "spur-of-the-moment" choice, somewhat like our impulse buying that we often later regret?

12. Read Eph. 1:3-14. What words in this section show that God's decision to "buy" us was no spur-of-the-moment impulse purchase? (Hint: see verses 4, 5, 9, 11.)

13. Read Rom. 8:38-39. What words in verse 39 give us comfort when we might be tempted to doubt that God still wants us?

14. What repeated words in Ps. 136 teach the same truth, namely, that we can continue to be assured that God will not change His mind?

15. Even when our conscience and heart condemn us, to whom, according to 1 John 3:20, should we turn? Why?

Titus 2:14 reminds us that Christ "gave Himself for us to redeem us from all iniquity *and* to purify for Himself a people of His own who are zealous for good deeds." The purpose was that we might belong to Him *and* serve Him. Just as we purchase an item to fill some need and serve some purpose, so God has purchased us to serve a purpose.

16. According to John 15:16, for what purpose did He choose us?

17. In 2 Cor. 5:15 what is the intention of Christ's death?
18. Why would most Christians tend to answer, "To save me," to the question, Why did Jesus die?
19. According to Eph. 2:10, for what purpose have we been made new in Christ?
20. Read Rom. 12:1. What response should the mercies of God arouse in us?
21. Read Rom. 6:3-13. For what purpose are we united with Christ in His death?
22. What is the purpose of our being united with Christ in His resurrection?
23. Verse 11 asks us to consider ourselves "alive to God." How do we demonstrate this in our lives?
24. List some ways we use our members as God's instruments of righteousness as verse 13 asks us to do. (See Matt. 25:34-40.)
25. What are we asked to do according to James 1:26-27?
26. According to John 13:34-35, what is to guide all our actions?

God has indeed given great worth to your life by the price He paid to purchase you in order to make you His own and also by allowing you to serve Him. We are indeed precious in the sight of God.

During each day of this week, read Rom. 6 and consciously seek to serve God. Be prepared at the beginning of the next lesson to discuss your experience as God's royal servant.

A Life That Has Been Enabled to Serve Him

The Holy Spirit within You

Far too often we hear Christians, when asked to witness, saying, "Oh, I can't do that!" Sometimes Christians say, "I wish I could give more." The truth of the matter is—we could probably do both.

At times people don't really want to do something, and so they hide behind the excuse of inability. Sometimes the "spirit is willing but the flesh is weak." At other times, we may be thoroughly convinced that we can't do it.

Today's lesson seeks to help you realize that a life alive unto God is a life that has been enabled to serve Him. The first part of 1 Cor. 6:19, which tells us that we have the Holy Spirit within us, makes it clear that we are able to serve Him.

1. What is the apostle Paul's confidence according to Phil. 4:13?
2. What are we promised in 2 Cor. 9:8?
3. Why do we, in light of such Scriptural assurances, so often hesitate?
4. What warning does Jesus give in John 15:5 concerning human efforts?
5. What is the significance of the statement "Your body is a temple of the Holy Spirit"?
6. In the light of the promise in Acts 2:38, when did you receive the Holy Spirit?
7. If we can sincerely call Jesus "Lord" (the sovereign we love and willingly follow), what assurance does 1 Cor. 12:3 give us?
8. If you are led to walk in the ways of the Spirit, what assurance does Rom. 8:14 and Gal. 5:17-18 give you?

9. What fruit does the Spirit produce in the lives of Christians? (See Gal. 5:22-23.)
10. According to Gal. 5:17, what goes on inside of the child of God?
11. How does that affect living a life alive unto God?
12. What comfort do we derive from the words of 1 John 1:7?

Jesus told His followers, "I tell you the truth: it is to your advantage that I go away, for if I do not go away, the Counselor will not come to you; but if I go, I will send Him to you" (John 16:7). It is evident that the disciples became changed men after Pentecost, the day the Holy Spirit was given to them.

13. According to the prophecy of Acts 1:8, to what can we attribute the change?
14. What did they receive from the Holy Spirit?
15. The Spirit's mighty work was manifested in believers of both the Old and New Testaments; who, according to Acts 10:38, received the Spirit and His power?
16. According to Luke 4:1, what happened to Jesus as He began His public ministry?
17. In 1 Peter 1:2 the effect that the Holy Spirit, who dwells in us, has on the chosen ones is described. What does the passage declare that the Spirit does?
18. To what end are we sanctified?
19. According to Phil. 2:13, what two things does God work in us?
20. If we feel that "we just can't serve the Lord," what does such contention say about this Bible passage?
21. Titus 3:5 tells us that two things have happened to the Christian: "regeneration" and "renewal in the Holy Spirit." Discuss what effect this has on your life.
22. The Titus passage undoubtedly refers to Baptism. What means of grace is described in 1 Peter 1:23 as giving new life?
23. According to 1 Thess. 2:13, the Word continues to be at work in those who already believe. What can it do? (Hint: see 1 Peter 2:2 and John 15:2-3.)
24. In Heb. 4:2 we are told what causes the Word to be of no benefit to the hearer. What is it?
25. If the Word doesn't have the promised effect on our lives, where does the fault lie?
26. The Holy Spirit, using the means of grace, works faith in us. How-

ever, not everyone who hears the message believes. According to Acts 7:51, what accounts for this?

God has given the Holy Spirit to those who belong to Him. Using the Word and the Sacraments, the Holy Spirit enables us to live for God. Is it possible for us, however, to ignore or resist the Spirit?

During the week, consciously seek to step out boldly, trusting in the promises of God. Be like Peter, who got out of the boat and walked to Jesus. But remember to keep your eyes on Christ lest you begin to sink.

Next week be prepared to share with the class members at least one occasion when you "stepped out in faith" during this week and dared to do something for the Lord. Describe how it felt to dare to do what you had not done before.

A Life Dedicated to Living to His Glory
Glorify God in Your Body

Most of us would be incensed if someone were to rob us. The more valuable and important to our plans the item is, the more upset we are if someone takes it from us. When that object of great value is stolen only to be misused or abused, we are even more upset. Let's relate that feeling to 1 Cor. 6:19-20.

We are God's property—made by Him and purchased with the holy, innocent suffering and death of Jesus Christ. We were specifically picked and chosen to accomplish great things for God. He has chosen to rest His whole plan of salvation, for which Christ gave so much, on those whom He has made His own. If we Christians were no longer to share the Gospel, it would "all go down the tube." As far as we know God has made no contingency plans.

The key phrase that directs our thoughts today is the last part of 1 Cor. 6:20: "So glorify God in your body."

1. What words from 1 Cor. 6:19 indicate that we are *able* to glorify God in our body?

2. What words from verse 19 indicate why we *ought* to glorify God in our body?

3. What words from verse 20 indicate why we *want* to glorify God in our body?

4. According to John 16:14, what is the task of the Spirit of truth?

5. If this same Spirit dwells in us, what will be His aim in our lives?

6. Another passage that speaks about belonging to God is 1 Peter 2:9.

What does our unique position as God's special people require of us?

7. According to Eph. 1:12, to what were the followers of Christ destined and appointed?

8. Read 1 Cor. 10:31. What is to be the purpose of *everything* we do?

It is easy to say we ought to and we are able to glorify God, but then comes the actual doing. Merely to talk in generalities about glorifying God without getting specific or actually doing it is useless.

9. What were the people mentioned in Mark 7:6 doing?

10. What was wrong with the honor given by their lips?

11. About what did the Lord warn in Luke 6:46?

12. According to Matt. 5:16, in what specific way are we to glorify God?

13. List one specific deed that would glorify God and share and discuss it with the class.

14. What specific deed is mentioned in Prov. 3:9 by which we can honor God?

15. In what way does the giving of firstfruits honor God? What statement do we make by first giving to God?

16. What did the offering referred to in 2 Cor. 9:12 accomplish besides helping the poor?

17. According to 1 Peter 4:10-11, what is to be the result of faithful stewardship?

There is no doubt that we ought and are able to give thanks. But before that happens we must be motivated to action. One can be motivated by threats and fear or by hope of reward (gaining some advantage), but seeking to honor and glorify God with such motives is hardly acceptable.

18. To what does the apostle Paul appeal in Rom. 12:1 when urging complete dedication of the whole life?

19. Some people place the motivation in our love for God. Where does 1 John 4:19 place the motivation?

20. At what time, according to Rom. 5:8, can we find God loving us and demonstrating that love for us?

21. Read Eph. 1:3-6. When did God's love and action on our behalf begin?

Christians dare not be children of God only at certain times and in certain areas of life. Our relation to God requires us to be wholly sanctified to Him, so that His glory is promoted by all we are and do. This includes the total person: soul and body, thoughts and desires, words and actions.

Rather than rob God of what is precious and important to Him, let us dedicate our lives to living to His glory. Who wants to serve and glorify the devil? Jesus reminds us, "No one can serve two masters. . . . You cannot serve God and mammon" (Matt. 6:24).

Make a list of the class members. During the week pray for each one by name, asking God to help them glorify Him with their lives.